HIGH SCHOOLS

HIGH SCHOOLS

TODAY AND TOMORROW

Charles W. Bursch and John Lyon Reid

 REINHOLD PUBLISHING CORPORATION

NEW YORK

Acknowledgment is made
with grateful thanks
for the efforts of:

Neil R. Penry
Thomas N. Echternach
Walter R. Bell
Thaddeus M. Nastich
Christopher Arnold, A.R.I.B.A.
Charles W. Bursch II, Ed.D.
Roy B. Bursch, M.A.

And particularly:
Ruby Bursch
Lilya Reid

CONTENTS

To Dr. Walter D. Cocking,

whose leadership in education has inspired America

High School Education under Critical Scrutiny

The high school of tomorrow, if it is to serve youth better than it does today, will find pupils at work on individualized schedules in place of class schedules. The individualized approach will be determined by the best known guidance practices and will be geared to the growth and development needs of each pupil.

The home base for each pupil will be an individual work station appropriately designed for a wide variety of learning activities and will be located close to a materials center and practical workshop. This will replace the corridor locker and the tablet armchair in a "home-room" generally occupied for a few minutes each day for roll-taking, school announcements, and a bit of group guidance.

It will find staff members serving as consultants and advisors to pupils as well as purveyors of specialized information. It will provide a rich choice of learning activities appropriate to each pupil as determined by an adequately staffed guidance service that will supplement the findings of home-room teacher-counselors. These learning activities will occur off campus as well as on, depending upon where the learning will be more realistic and thus more meaningful to pupils.

In such a setting, the authors of this book do not feel presumptuous in making this somewhat startling proposal — a program dominated by a truly individualized schedule as opposed to one dominated by a class schedule.

While seeming new, the proposal developed here deals primarily with the implementation of previous proposals which analyzed the purposes of high school education, curriculum and co-curriculum content, psychological factors of learning, staff competence and attitudes, pupil guidance, and length of class periods. But progress in the implementation of these proposals has been distressingly slow.

This slowness is caused largely by three things: fixed class-schedule domination of the program, unsuitability of the high school plant to implement the proposals, and unwillingness to adjust procedures and plant provisions in order to make full use of community resources.

What can be done with high school scheduling and the high school plant in order to implement current efforts to revise the educational offering and methods of teaching in high school? That is the central theme of this book.

Role of the High School

An important responsibility of any society is the induction of its young people into adult life in such a way that their behavior will be mature. In America, it has become traditional to assign much of this responsibility to the high schools. The high school has been and is now one of the key instruments in realizing the American dream of the good life by training teen-age boys and girls in competent, responsible citizenship. The task is national in scope and crucial in significance.

It has become axiomatic in America that all teen-agers are entitled to a high school education of good quality and that this opportunity must be made available. In fact, the national welfare requires that we, the senior citizens, make sure that we are doing everything possible to make our high schools a true training ground for literate and competent citizenry.

It has also been well established that the governmental unit responsible for the educational function is the state. Each state is charged by the Constitution with the responsibility for providing an adequate legal, organizational, and financial structure for the accomplishment of the task. The state, however, has assigned to the local district the administrative responsibility for providing high school educational facilities.

It is up to each school district to produce the wherewithal for the young people's education, or, in the event it cannot because state laws or an inadequate tax base prevents, to advise state and federal educational officials and the state legislatures and Congress of the inadequacies.

There is ample evidence, reported by nationally recognized economists, that America's income is sufficiently great to finance high quality programs and plants for our high schools. It remains, in numerous instances, for the necessary funds to be authorized and the burden for providing them to be fairly distributed.

Changes Considered

Although educational needs have not remained static, ways of meeting them have, in far too many of our high schools. For many years now, people — educators and laymen alike — who are interested in the improvement of education have clearly recognized that it is time for a major overhaul of teaching methods, scheduling, class size, curriculum, and plant.

A number of basic factors have led to an intensive search for less costly ways of providing a high school education. Outstanding among these factors are the great impact of burgeoning post-war enrollments, the recurrent fruitless search for well qualified teachers in sufficient numbers, and the losing battle for necessary plant.

12

The pressure to reduce costs has temporarily cooled the ardor of some of the people who had been working for program improvement. Increasingly it is a serious question whether even the quality of high school education to which the community is accustomed can be maintained.

Various proposals for reducing costs have been offered. Typical are increased class size, larger schools, reduced educational offering (a return to the teaching of alleged fundamentals), earlier school-leaving age for those not academically inclined, and an eleven- or twelve-month school year. Most of these suggestions are soon abandoned because they are found to be obviously untenable when checked against the determination of an aroused public to improve the education of the teen-agers.

There are also proposals to reduce the costs of high school education by spending less on sites, buildings, and equipment. These suggestions not only include smaller areas and cheaper land for sites, but also the use of standard plans and specifications, temporary buildings, and less costly heating, ventilating, plumbing, and hardware installations. These specific school plant "economy" proposals are receiving more serious and sustained consideration than are those to reduce costs in matters directly involving teachers, pupils, and curriculum.

The willingness to go along with reduced quality in school plant at the same time that an improvement in the quality of the educational program is being sought is generally based upon a superficial analysis of what is involved.

The trite assertion "good buildings do not make a good program" is taken by some people to mean that the nature and quality of the plant is not directly related to the nature and quality of the educational program. This kind of reasoning, when accepted, results in placing poorly planned and poorly equipped temporary buildings on inadequate sites.

Such a procedure constitutes false economy and is a barrier to desired revisions in high school education. It is not possible to make many of the desired improvements in curriculum, methods, and procedures in the type of high school plant commonly found today. Such plants must be substantially retooled if a new program is to succeed. By the same token, new sites and installations must be specifically selected, planned, and arranged to meet new educational requirements.

When changes occur in method or content of an educational program, a different kind of plant is needed. For example, a teacher station for a classroom used for formal instruction and discussion is a desk and chair at the front of the room and is backed by a teacher's chalkboard. In many sections of America this arrangement is still meeting local needs as they have been met for several generations.

In a program characterized by pupils working independently and in small committee-like groups, the teacher station must be an office-like room for consultations with pupils. Pupil work stations in this program must be something more than a tablet-arm chair. Furthermore, it is essential to provide space and furniture suitable for committees to work in semi-privacy.

A most dramatic illustration of the need for completely different facilities for a different educational concept is found in the homemaking department. When education in this field proceeds upon the basis that homemaking is an integrated and unified whole, the laboratory required is quite different from the separate and highly specialized food and clothing laboratories now found in most high schools.

The school district has made an expensive choice, indeed, when it adopts a plant program that results in buildings — no matter how cheaply constructed — which hinder the progress of the desired educational improvement. The few dollars per pupil per year — the maximum that can be saved — constitute but a very small fraction of the annual per pupil outlay for all educational costs except plant.

It is no wonder that the high school is subjected to continuous evaluation and criticism. In recent years, that criticism has become sharper and more prevalent. Paralleling the increased criticism, there have been competent, well organized, and widespread attempts to improve the high school's effectiveness. It is unfortunate that these attempts have not been more successful. Even where they have been tried, their success has been piecemeal and spotty, whereas the situation requires basic changes, and, in effect, complete overhaul. This is, indeed, the constant refrain among those who discuss the problem.

Educators are not the only ones aware of current high school program inadequacies. Zealous parent groups and citizens' committees are giving a great deal of attention to the matter, and their concern has become the concern of state and national governments. All agencies identified with youth and with the control of juvenile delinquency have labeled inadequacies in high school programs as contributors to what is known as "the youth problem."

Manpower commissions and large employers have put the finger on inadequate high school education as one of the principal sources of the serious imbalance in manpower demand and supply. They have found that this is especially true in jobs that require mathematics, science, and other technical skills. In addition, employers have also deplored the lack in many high school graduates of self-reliance, sense of responsibility, and ability to get along with others.

Great numbers of pupils reject the current programs. This is evidenced by the large percentage that drop out as soon as the compulsory attendance laws will permit, and sooner if it can be accomplished without too great a penalty.

Until quite recently, the plant has not been deeply involved in the general criticism of the effectiveness of the high school. Currently, however, an increasing number of people are recognizing the critical importance of the plant in program improvement. This recognition, along with the enormous volume of high school construction now going on and that will be required during the next decade, plus the natural permanence and relative inflexibility of this plant, has brought it into sharp focus. The tenor of comment on the high school buildings erected in recent years is that they are educationally obsolete when occupied. They are designed largely for a program which is being seriously challenged and which, in many instances, is undergoing drastic modification.

Taking Stock of the Present
Program and Plant

There are many factors to be considered in the evaluation of a high school program. A few transcend the others in over-all importance:

1. The relationship between the program offered and the currently-accepted goals to be attained. These must be clearly understood by both teachers and pupils.
2. The curricular organization and content, the learning procedures used, and the scheduling of pupil's work. These must be clearly related to the prevailing goals.
3. What is known about the learning process and the growth and development of youth. This knowledge must be applied consistently throughout the school.
4. The program of the high school. It must have a recognized significance to all students.
5. Organization and scheduling of work, and assignment of the teaching staff. These must be more responsive to the needs and characteristics of the individual pupil than to the requirements of the class, the group, the school as a whole, the subject matter involved, or the pressures of special interest groups within our society.

Many high school programs are found wanting when considered on the basis of these factors, even though most of them are making significant efforts to improve.

It is somewhat simpler to determine whether or not the criticism that new high school plants are educationally obsolete when occupied is justified. Two questions are raised: Does the plant implement the educational program now approved and operating? Is the plant designed for future inexpensive alterations?

A school plant that does not, throughout its life, implement a desirable educational program is worse than merely a waste of money. It results in hobbling the effectiveness of the much larger annual per pupil expenditure for non-capital outlays.

The presence of an inappropriate school plant may explain why changes in the educational program are not more often undertaken or, when attempted, do not work out satisfactorily.

Program   High school programs vary so much that, in a way, they defy general description. Evaluation of a single high school is easily done, but to do this for all high schools is quite another matter. Regardless of what might be said, it could not be entirely true of any one school. However, there are some common characteristics. Most high schools have:

1. The school day divided into class periods varying in duration from forty to sixty minutes.
2. Each period devoted to a "subject" such as English, mathematics, social studies, or chemistry. Many of these are required for graduation or for college entrance.
3. Each subject taught by a teacher with credentials to teach that particular subject.
4. Evaluation of, and grades given for, students' work in these subjects in terms of ground covered and comprehension of the contents of the course. This places a high value on mediocrity. The bright pupils will often do no more than required and, in turn, the amount of work required is conditioned by what the less-bright pupils can accomplish.
5. A social program administered in such a way as to interfere least with the daily schedule of courses.
6. A student body government operating upon a pattern substantially dictated by school officials.
7. A formal or informal guidance service concerned primarily with assisting students in the selection of courses or course patterns. These selections are justified on the basis of preparation for future duties and responsibilities of citizenship, college, a vocation, and adult life in general. The guidance service, therefore, is one in which adults decide what courses should be taken by the students and when they should be taken. This type of guidance places an emphasis upon what the adults think ought to be done instead of upon what is currently significant to pupils.
8. An administrative attitude of complete responsibility for and control of pupils. This results in the attachment of great importance to attendance at classes, formalities in securing library privileges, and units of credit. This attitude and these controls establish the average high school as a center for the care, control, and formal education of youth, a center substantially separate from the ebb and flow of community life. This

youth-center concept results in a high school program and plant where-in pupils are to be protected from community life until they are ready, at some later date, to enter it. In actuality, youth constitutes a substantial and vital segment of community life. Full recognition of this in terms of school practice gives vitality to all educational effort.

How do these characteristics measure up to the factors given at the beginning of this chapter?

The division of the school day into class periods during which subjects — most of them required — are taught by specialist teachers results in an adult or school-determined arrangement to which a pupil must conform. This type of setting makes it easy for the school to impose upon the pupil what it thinks is good for him but difficult for it to respond to the needs and interests of the individual.

The almost universal practice of grading pupils competitively on the amount of work covered in a course, and the amount of information retained, makes it difficult to relate subject matter to individual interests and needs and to the concept of pupil growth and development. The tacit but mostly erroneous assumption prevails that doing well in a given course is evidence of growth. Here again, the school is more concerned with what the pupil does to the subject matter than with what the subject matter does to and for the pupil.

Social programs in high school and student body governments often reflect the philosophy that these things are extra-curricular and therefore should be available only to those who turn in a good academic performance. At any rate, they should not be permitted to interfere with the "real" purpose of education, namely, subject matter proficiency.

It is true that many schools have moved toward actual integration of so-called curricular and extra-curricular activities. The wide use of the word "co-curriculum" shows progress along this line. This is all to the good, but as long as a division is recognized, the growth-development concept of learning is discredited to some degree.

Educational guidance services offered in high schools differ markedly in point of view, scope, and competence, but they have one type of limitation in common. The redirection of pupils' educational efforts, when justified, is limited too much to the educational offering of the school. Basically, educational guidance stops with the counsel that certain courses be taken and that others be avoided. To be effective in a growth-development pattern, guidance must be able to offer something more in accord with individual need than the taking of a subject.

When the high school is envisioned as a youth center where society provides preparation for effective participation in adult life, it is necessary to insist upon certain courses. It is also necessary for administrators and teachers to assume responsibility for seeing that lessons are actually prepared. However, when the growth-development approach to learning is used and when developmental tasks for pupils are being sought, the youth center idea is no longer tenable. Basic and obvious integration of all learning with community life becomes imperative. Sense of reality and significance of the learning task become essential characteristics.

Only to a limited extent can this be realized when a student finds himself in an institution for youth, even though the avowed purpose of that institution is to prepare youth for adult life. Young people have a compelling interest in participating in real life activities, but a very limited and erratic interest in preparing for some possible eventuality. Preparation for adult life is best attained by participation in life, but not so well by becoming proficient in academic disciplines, the usefulness of which may become apparent only at some later time.

Although a high degree of competence in academic subjects is often an absolute necessity, it should be pointed out that effort to teach this competence to unready pupils is worse than wasted. It warps personalities and develops pupils' dislike for school.

The complexities involved in any evaluation of the high school's educational program are emphasized by the apparent paradoxes involved in its criticisms.

We often hear that one fault with the high school is college domination of the curriculum, yet colleges are frequently the severest critics of the high school because its graduates are not ready to proceed with college work. Since most high schools have made a serious effort to prepare pupils for college on a pattern largely dictated by colleges, it appears that both colleges and high schools should be willing to try a different approach to college preparation. Some of them, in fact, are doing just that. There is evidence that high school pupils prepared in a growth and development pattern do as well or better in college than do those who are prepared in a traditional pattern. Success of high school graduates in college might be further enhanced if colleges as well as high schools gave more attention to the laws of learning and to activities designed for the growth and development of pupils.

A second paradox is that some critics clamor that high schools are too subject-matter conscious, while others say that the graduates are incompetent in the basic skills. Here again, it appears that it is not sufficient for the high school merely to try harder to teach the so-called fundamentals. Fundamentals learned as an essential part of a task that has vital and immediate significance to the pupil presents an attractive way to solve this problem.

Thirdly, some critics claim that high school courses bore pupils because they are too difficult. Others hold that high school education holds no challenge to pupils because its courses are too easy — and have no hard core to be mastered.

In the face of these conflicting criticisms, high schools have offered watered-down or snap courses. Repeated drives have also been conducted to stiffen academic requirements and to increase academic performance. These attempted solutions have been only partially effective.

Young people who see no point in doing difficult tasks but who, for various reasons, cannot or do not wish to drop out of school, naturally seek the least painful path — the snap course. The fact that many of these young people are bored is not closely related to the difficulty of the work but to its lack of significance to them. There has been a common belief that it is the technical difficulty of some courses that causes dislike of them. This, of course, has validity for the less able students, but an easy course can be just as boring and just as offensive as a too difficult one if it deals with matters that are not related to the felt needs of pupils.

High school buildings, as well as educational programs and administrative **Plant** patterns, vary a great deal. No general description of plant could apply in a single building. But here again, as in the case of the educational program, it is desirable to describe the usual plant type.

A predominance of small academic classrooms. The design of these classrooms reflects an emphasis upon class work rather than upon individual or small group activities. Minimum floor space per pupil, absence of running water, remote access to the out-of-doors, amount and type of storage space, kind of student stations — all reveal an emphasis upon verbalization, upon figuring, and upon viewing and listening as the principal learning activities. There are no satisfactory provisions for individual or small-group projects that involve hand work, role-playing, dramatics, and other types of active pupil participation and problem-solving.

Formalized science laboratories. Each of these is designed for teacher demonstration and each has a type of student station suitable for carrying out a series of prescribed formal experiments required of all pupils. Missing from this type of laboratory is provision for the pursuit of a pupil's special interest in science. Facilities for a pupil to work upon a project over an extended period are either inappropriate or lacking. Floor space is limited to that needed for a specified number of work stations. No space is available for projects which require construction or assemblies too large to be accommodated on top of a laboratory table.

Industrial arts, home arts, and vocational shops and laboratories. These are designed for classwork but also have provisions which permit a high degree of individualization of work projects. Many of these shop spaces are designed to accommodate work on a wide variety of individual projects. Furthermore, provision is usually made for storage of tools, equipment, and materials. Shops and laboratories for vocational agriculture best facilitate

21

individual projects that have real significance and vitality because of their relationship to home and community. Other areas of high school education have much to learn from vocational education in providing a plant that can accommodate individualized programs.

Library. The library consists mainly of a large reading room which is often lined with bookshelves. There are also book stacks, an alcove for periodicals, a librarian's control desk and facilities, and a librarian's work room. Sometimes an audio-visual aids center is part of this room. In such a situation, audio-visual aids and equipment are stored, controlled, and distributed from the library. This type of high school library is designed primarily to serve pupils who come to it and remain during the time books and periodicals are used. Its justification goes back to a time when the daily schedules of pupils called for about as many study or library periods as class periods. The trend today in scheduling is to assign pupils to classes for most of the day. Opportunities for pupils to go to the library are therefore distinctly limited. An individualized educational program would increase greatly the opportunities for pupils to use the library. It would also increase the need for the library to provide book cart service to pupil groups wherever they may be working on campus. Audio-visual aids centers operated in conjunction with the library illustrate what must be done on a much more inclusive basis in order to meet the needs of pupils in an individualized program. In such a program, the library and audio-visual aids center would become but part of a complete materials center and curricular laboratory.

An auditorium or speech arts center. It is designed and equipped for dramatics, assemblies, lectures, debates, music instruction,and performance. The auditorium often takes the form of a little theatre, while larger, less formal meetings are held in rally courts, outdoor theatres, or in the gymnasium. These facilities for auditorium and dramatics are often unsuitable for a teacher-dominated formalized type of instruction and performance in speech arts and pupil-project approach to speech arts and dramatics. With the pupil-project approach, the students need a wider choice in stage arrangements. They need a more open type of stage area with stage-craft facilities adjoining. The stage and stage-craft area must be constructed of materials which permit revisions during the process of working out various projects.

An administration center. This contains offices for the administrative, supervisory, guidance, and clerical staffs, teachers' restrooms, work rooms, and sometimes a conference room and professional library. Often located here are student body offices and space for staff members of student publications. Administration quarters such as these serve quite well for an educational program operated under the concept that the principal is boss of the school and his supervisors help to maintain academic standards. However, in an educational program which places great emphasis upon individual needs, the administration services become but a part of a larger group of educational services housed in a school service center. In this center, would be found the school library, staff library, curricular laboratory, visual aids, models, construction materials, communication facilities, student body quarters, as well as the quarters for the guidance and administrative staff.

A food service center. This includes kitchen, food service area, students' main lunch room, and one small group lunch room each for faculty and student groups. The lunch rooms are frequently designed for uses other than food service, generally as social rooms. Providing adequate feeding services to a school where the educational program is individualized is not a substantially different problem from providing them in a school dominated by class schedules. The social and recreational aspects of the feeding facilities, however, become more important in the individualized program because the periodic and valuable opportunities for pupil intermingling on a school-wide basis is curtailed in the individual schedule program.

A physical education center. It is usually dominated by a gymnasium designed for basketball as a spectator sport. A girls' gymnasium is also provided in high schools of large enrollment. Shower and dressing rooms for each sex and office space for physical education coaches and instructors adjoin the main gymnasium room. Sometimes there are separate rooms for corrective exercises, tumbling, boxing, wrestling, and other activities. Also, at times, a swimming pool is included. Quite elaborate outdoor facilities are usually provided. Fields and courts for football, soccer, baseball, softball, tennis, basketball, and volleyball are common, as are also a running track and provisions for field events. Spectator space is seldom omitted from the football and baseball fields and the running track. The physical education and recreational facilities for a school in which individual work schedules prevail should not differ substantially in kind from those found in a typical high school today. They should, however, differ in the emphasis placed upon some types of activities. Quarters for staff members, for instance, would be designed for pupil consultation rather than primarily as a staff work and record space. Substantial differences in space-provision emphasis should also occur as a result of use by the pupils of recreation facilities throughout the community and not limited to school hours. An individualized program would also make greater demands upon corrective facilities and upon activities such as golf, bowling, fishing, and others having lifelong significance for active recreation.

Student traffic arteries and exits. These are designed to carry the peak requirements occurring at the close of each class period or an assembly call or fire drill. Placed along the sides of the traffic lanes, or grouped just off these lanes at strategic points, are individual lockers for storage and protection of pupil's clothes, books, and other personal belongings. School corridors have been well designed to meet student traffic problems of present programs. Their adequacy has been a concern not only of educators and of architects but of fire and panic authorities armed with police power for enforcing standards. The patterns of pupil traffic in a school with individualized work schedules would, during most of the day, differ from those operating under a more traditional program. The traffic jam between each class period would disappear. However, a similar congestion might occur at the noon hour, at the close of the school day, and when a general assembly or rally is called. Student lockers in the individualized program would be in the home-room station of the pupil. This would reduce the traffic congestion caused by locker placement in corridors. The net effect upon corridor design for an individualized program should be to reduce the amount of building area devoted to student traffic.

All in all, high school plants have been well designed to implement traditional programs. Some recent high school buildings reflect educators' desires to make the educational program informal and geared to the individual. Only on extremely rare occasions have high school plants been designed with sufficient flexibility to meet major changes in program or procedure.

Classrooms and laboratories with greater floor area; conference rooms adjoining classrooms, laboratories, and libraries; a greater proportion of the building area devoted to social activities and student body enterprises; these illustrate the results of such attempts. So far as we know, however, there has been no complete high school plant designed to meet the requirements of a program which operates on individual pupil schedules rather than on the prevailing class schedules. Exploration of the design requirements of such a school is one of the purposes of this book.

3

Efforts for Improvement Examined

Many things are being done to improve high school education. The common purposes discernable in these efforts are to make the educational offering more significant to the pupils and the work of the school more efficient, i.e., to accomplish more with a given amount of time and effort.

One group, the Educational Policies Commission, representing the National Education Association and the American Association of School Administrators, undertook some years ago to state clearly and succinctly the educational needs of youth in America today. The Commission's summary of ten imperative educational needs of all youth, first published in 1944,° has been instrumental in clarifying the task of the high school and in envisioning that task in its entirety and from the point of view of youth. Some of the strength and effectiveness of the statement stems from its expression of the needs of youth rather than from what the school should accomplish.

The ten point statement follows.

1. All youth need to develop salable skills and those understandings and attitudes that make the worker an intelligent and productive participant in economic life. To this end, most students need supervised work experience as well as education in the skills and knowledge of their occupations.
2. All youth need to develop and maintain good health and physical fitness.
3. All youth need to understand the rights and duties of the citizen in a democratic society, and to be intelligent and competent in the per-

Imperative Educational Needs of Youth

°*Education for All American Youth.* The Educational Policies Commission of the National Educational Association of the United States and the American Association of School Administrators. Washington, D. C., 1944, 1952, p. 216

25

formance of their obligations as members of the community and citizens of the state and nation.

4. All youth need to understand the significance of the family for the individual and society and the conditions conducive to successful family life.

5. All youth need to know how to purchase and use goods and services intelligently, understanding both the values received by the consumer and the economic consequences of their acts.

6. All youth need to understand the methods of science, the influence of science on human life, and the main scientific facts concerning the nature of the world and of man.

7. All youth need opportunities to develop their capacities to appreciate beauty in literature, art, music, and nature.

8. All youth need to be able to use their leisure time well and to budget it wisely, balancing activities that yield satisfactions to the individual with those that are socially useful.

9. All youth need to develop respect for other persons, to grow in their insight into ethical values and principles, and to be able to live and work cooperatively with others.

10. All youth need to grow in their ability to think rationally, to express their thoughts clearly, and to read and listen with understanding.

Paralleling the broadly based effort to define the educational needs of American youth is a similar effort to understand better the laws of learning and the growth and development patterns of high school children. One group of educators and psychologists has concentrated its research on stating pertinent principles, along with their most obvious implications for the physical plant. The results of this study, quite typical of the findings of others working in the same area, follow.

Some Principles of the Growth and Learning of High School Pupils

1. Youth need freedom in which to be active physically as a way of learning, of sustaining interest and minimizing fatigue, boredom, and irritability. Therefore, we need to plan for space and equipment that will permit freedom of activity.

2. To teach effectively, teachers need a great deal of information about each individual. They must not only know him well but be able to observe him in a variety of activities throughout the day. The pupil too needs a sustained relationship with his teacher. Identification with the teacher created by the feeling he is understood and liked facilitates learning. Therefore, we must make provisions for a self-contained or laboratory type classroom.

3. Youth learn attitudes, information, and skills from one another. When they are given opportunities to interact, learning is accelerated because the sources of teaching are increased. Smaller group and committee

work help all youth to develop the social skills which are important to their present development as well as to their future as citizens. Therefore, equipment should be flexible and conducive to working in large and small groups.

4. Curiosity about the physical environment and physical phenomena is a strong and continuing motivation for learning. Youth need many opportunities to explore the environment, to observe the growth of plants and animals, and to experiment as a way of developing a scientific point of view. Therefore, the plant should permit easy exit to the out-of-doors, provisions for care of plants and animals, and facilities for experiments.

5. Accurate concepts develop through concrete experiences in which youth construct and handle tangible objects and models. The meanings derived from reading and discussion must continually be verified and extended through such activities as experimentation, construction, painting, drawing, dramatic play, and rhythms. Therefore, classrooms should provide space for construction, dramatic play, etc., and provision for display of models, globes, objects.

6. Youth need many opportunities to work independently as well as in groups and to develop their individual interests. Each pupil's interests, growing out of his own experience and his own unique abilities give him persistent motivation for learning, enrich his leisure time and influence his future vocational choices. Therefore arrangements for individual work and flexible interest centers should be made.*

The work of the First and Second Commissions of Life Adjustment Education for Youth supplies concrete evidence of the recognition of a widespread need for major improvement in high school education, and of equally widespread efforts to develop an action program that will bring about the improvement.

There is more than ordinary significance in the work of these two commissions. They were constituted upon a broad professional base and held the view that what secondary education needed most was an action program for improvement. They called national attention to the evidence of this need, and pointed with emphasis to the evident neglect by the schools of their obligation to the graduates who do not go to college or who do not plan to enter a skilled occupation.

The deplorable over-all condition revealed by the 1947-48 findings of the First Commission was that "only about seven youth out of ten enter senior high school and fewer than five of them remain to graduate."

*Prepared under the direction of Sybil Richardson, Consultant, Division of Research and Guidance, County of Los Angeles, Los Angeles, California

The First Commission looked to the state departments of education to take leadership in stimulating improvement programs in high school districts.

At a later date — 1953 — twenty-nine of the forty-eight states responded to a United States Office of Education questionnaire designed to discover activities "which seemed to have pertinence to the growth of life adjustment education" and to learn "about the road blocks which might be retarding the improvements needed in secondary education."

In a United States Office of Education Bulletin entitled *A Look Ahead in Secondary Education*,° the Second Commission on Life Adjustment Education for Youth described the improvement programs reported by the twenty-nine states and projected the continuing aspects of such a program. In this projection, the Second Commission's report (pages 84-90) lists the following items of unfinished business:

1. The secondary school staffs need to continue their studies of all youth, but especially those now tending to drop out before graduation.
2. Educators are working to establish a 14-year sequence of educational experience, which will eliminate the selective character of secondary education.
3. In terms of time allotment, an appropriate balance between required and and elective subjects or areas of learning has not been adequately determined.
4. Continuing experimentation is needed to provide for greater individualization in instruction by a wide range of methods.
5. There is need for more experimentation to build a program of work experience.
6. An adequate program for appraising the educational development of individual pupils needs to be developed.
7. Secondary school teachers and principals have a contribution to make toward improving programs of teacher preparation.
8. The problem of school finance remains critical even after the adoption of State equalization programs.
9. The whole question of home-community-school responsibility should be re-examined.

It is the purpose of this book to explore the implications of school plant design for a high school educational program that meets these challenges.

°*A Look Ahead in Secondary Education*, United States Office of Education Bulletin, No. 4, 1954. U. S. Dept. of Health, Education, and Welfare, Washington 25, D. C.

Current Status and Future Promise

of Improvement Efforts

4

Efforts to improve high school education have in recent years been focused primarily upon making it more appropriate to its professed purposes, more significant to youth, more in line with the principles of growth, development, and learning, and consequently more efficient in terms of the returns to society for the money expended. Any complete appraisal of current status reveals both outstanding successes and glaring failures.

The successes have been in the formulation of statements of philosophy, of educational needs, and of direction for progress. Through research and experimentation, great strides have been made in understanding better the laws of learning and the principles of growth and development. The need for guidance services is now almost as well recognized as is the need for instruction, even though the problems and financing of staff and facilities for the service have not been worked out altogether satisfactorily.

The special educational needs of those who will not attend college have been universally recognized, with the result that new courses have been designed to meet them. In numerous instances, working agreements have been reached whereby colleges accept pupils who have not completed the traditional college entrance pattern of high school subjects. These arrangements keep college opportunities open to young people who, during part or all of their high school career, didn't plan to attend college. Such arrangements also give high schools an opportunity to permit individuals in the college entrance group to deviate from a rigid course requirement pattern.

Another evidence of improvement occurs in the field of co-curricular activities. These activities have been greatly increased in variety and enrichment and have had more school time allotted to them. They have become a vital part of the school curriculum.

One of the attacks upon the academic type of high school program has been to vary the highly standardized class period allotment for each subject or course. This allotment of forty to sixty minutes is now often recognized as being entirely too brief for many learning experiences. Some high schools have provided longer class periods — usually double periods — in which combined courses, mostly social studies and English, have been offered. This arrangement has reduced the sharpness of artificial subject matter boundaries. It also provides opportunities for teachers of various subjects to work cooperatively and to use learning units, projects, and problem-solving methods instead of a more slavish use of text books. Furthermore, under this arrangement pupils and teachers get to know each other better, so that teachers can be more helpful in guidance and the pupils can have a more personalized identification with the school authorities.

Still another evidence of success is the substantial number of instances in which high school administrators, supervisors, and subject-matter teachers have worked together to clarify philosophy, revise curriculum, improve and informalize teaching and learning procedures, implement guidance, care for special individual needs, and broaden the basis for evaluation of pupils' work beyond mastery of subjects and measurement of skills.

The evidence of success, impressive as it is, is more than offset by the evidence of failure to accomplish the desired changes.

The fact cannot be evaded that there remains a frighteningly wide gap between most high school educational practices and the newer practices advocated by competent authorities. It is difficult to understand or condone this situation when the newer practices are accepted in principle by most high school administrators and other interested groups.

Many explanations have been advanced for the lack of greater progress in closing the existing gap. Most important are lack of adequate financing, unreadiness of teaching staff to accept training in methods of teaching, unwillingness of staff to reduce excessive subject-matter emphasis, and opposition of parents and taxpayers.

This impressive array of hurdles cannot and should not be minimized. They do suggest — perhaps require — that transition from the current approach to a new one be gradual. There is, however, at least one important consideration frequently lacking in the discussions of the hurdles encountered. This is the adverse influence of a traditional type high school plant.

This neglect is explained in many ways. Among these is a familiar but unjustified idea that if staff members have average competence, the right point of view, and sufficient determination, a good educational program can be had in any kind of plant. Another factor is the piecemeal approach. There has been a justifiable reluctance to spend large sums on retooling the plant for a modified program that was considered by many to be experimental. So much evidence now supports proposals for improving high school education that retooling the plant has become a wise investment. In fact, it is an investment that is an essential part of the improvement effort if gains are to be prompt, general, and permanent.

The almost universal finding is that the instructional portions of the new high schools are still basically designed for an academic emphasis. This is somewhat relieved in a few instances, where flexibility in design has made it comparatively easy and inexpensive to re-dimension interior spaces whenever required by program changes. It is pertinent at this point to explore the reasons for this condition.

Too many school authorities seem to feel that they are gambling building funds against the uncertainty of an improvement program. This attitude is apparent whether a new school is to be designed or an old one redesigned. Until school districts are willing to invest the necessary funds for making the plant ready for the proposed program changes, no real and lasting success can be expected.

To be sure, if a choice had to be made between a competent staff and an appropriate plant, the immediate benefit of youth would require that the choice be made in favor of the staff. However, it should be clearly understood that the new aims of education and new learning procedures cannot be satisfactorily attained in a traditionally designed high school. A plant designed to accommodate a closely scheduled basic program of class periods and a supplementary program of social and recreational activities, is not satisfactory for the new methods. Meeting individual needs, as determined by an adequate guidance service, and accommodating curriculum and learning experiences that are tailored to the individual rather than to the class and the daily schedule, requires a new approach to school design.

An important retardant to the improvement of education has been the compromises made necessary by trying to implement the traditional and the life-adjustment philosophies of education on the same campus.

The *traditional* approach has a relatively fixed curriculum and an even more rigid schedule of classes. Ground to be covered and time spent in classes are key concepts. In effect, this type of philosophy says to the student, "These are the subjects you must master and these the hours you must spend in the mastery." Failure on the part of some of the students to cover the ground satisfactorily is taken as evidence of lack of effort or lack of ability or both. These same students might have accomplished the purposes of the course by doing something other than attending a scheduled class, and might have needed a different time allotment.

Conventional design of high school buildings has implemented this type of approach. Most of the serious attempts at improving the traditional philosophy have proceeded on the basis of gradual change. This leaves the class period and the daily schedule concepts and practices relatively intact. The improvement consists principally of increased teacher effort for taking care of individual needs within the class-schedule framework. Any thorough-going implementation of the growth-development philosophy of education would require the subordination of class periods and fixed daily schedules to the educational needs of individual pupils.

The *growth-development* philosophy requires that groups — small or large — be formed and scheduled at a time, and for a duration, appropriate to the felt needs of the students composing the group. The class or committee grouping results from the guidance activities of the teaching and guidance staffs. Putting this philosophy into use requires, first of all, that each student have an individual schedule of work and an individual work station rather than an approved schedule of courses as a basis for belonging in the school. It is the absence in high school buildings of such individualized and committee type opportunities for each pupil that makes necessary the compromises which work to defeat the efforts toward improvement.

With the individual pupil station arrangement, the student's time would be spent in working individually upon matters related to his growth and development until he finds that he needs group work to move ahead more effectively.

When operating from an individual schedule of work and an individual work station, each student can schedule his own time effectively and also include conferences with the guidance staff, general teachers, or special resource teachers in library, in laboratory, or off the school grounds as the situation requires. Until class and committee groups can be formed to serve the needs of students at the time the need is felt and only for as long as needed, there is no real hope of substantially improving the high school educational program. Group instruction and work must be formed around specific needs of pupils as observed by staff members and as developed by advisory and guidance activities.

The fullest effectiveness of the learning process is realized when students are selected and grouped in terms of learning purposes. The techniques of grouping are complex. The basic consideration is that students be brought together when a common interest or purpose is discovered and be disbanded when that purpose is accomplished. Work and discussion proceed best when these groupings represent not only a common interest but also a cross section of individual traits which stimulate discussion and an interplay of ideas.

Thus, the common purpose which binds a group together may be fertilized by a range of individuals of differing social, economic, racial, and religious backgrounds. Our knowledge of the techniques of analyzing individuals and forming groups is not yet scientific or well developed. It is also true that for administrative convenience, groups once formed have traditionally been kept together longer than warranted by constructive learning results. The considerable body of data that is represented in the student records at the administrative and guidance center, and which is quickly available through

32

sorting machines, will make the formulation and reformulation of these groups a matter of considerable precision.

Provisions are made in all parts of the school plant for the quick and easy grouping and regrouping of students. In the building, heavy emphasis is given to spaces and rooms for groups of all sizes and for the varying activities of these groups.

A summary of the current status and future promise of efforts at improving the educational program in high schools reveals that substantial ground has been gained in curriculum supplementation, revision, and enrichment. Guidance activities have been increased and improved. A limited work experience educational program has been undertaken. The use of community resources, largely through class trips and visits, has become a part of the educational program in some schools.

However, a wide disparity exists between what competent educators say should be done and what is actually done in terms of accepted philosophy, recognized educational needs of youth, known growth and development patterns, and established laws of learning. Two important reasons for this disparity are selected for special consideration: a rigid administratively predetermined school day schedule, and a school plant geared to the rigid class schedule rather than to individual schedules of work. The correction of these deficiencies in high schools would create an environment which would invite the development of a high school educational program that conforms to the best in prevailing thought on education.

5

The Educational Program Proposed
for America's High Schools

So far, attention has been given to some of the shortcomings of today's typical high school program of education. Consideration has also been given to the nature and effectiveness of various efforts toward improvement. It now seems appropriate to set down some of the principal characteristics of an adequate educational program for America's high schools.

The matters of principal concern are:

1. Pupil *guidance* based upon adequate testing, data recording, and staff conference procedures
2. Availability of appropriate *content* in the form of units of work, problems, projects, lessons, and activities as well as texts, reference books, brochures, and pamphlets
3. Suitable opportunities for the development of *scholarship*
4. Suitable and adequate record-keeping and *evaluation* procedures
5. Proper *scheduling* and timing of learning activities
6. *Staffing* for assistance in the learning activity, in the testing, evaluation, and documentation of results
7. A *physical plant* that is most conducive to learning, and most efficient in terms of pupil and teacher time spent on units of learning

Guidance. The essence of an adequate educational program is finding and implementing desirable growth and development patterns for all youth. To be successful in this, the school must give prime consideration to the needs of individual pupils rather than to the establishment of classes and courses.

In such an individualized program, consultation, counseling, testing, evaluation, and achievement-accounting are activities that must take precedence over classroom instruction. There are questions that must be asked and answered initially for each pupil by the guidance process and re-examined whenever requested by the pupil or a school staff member. Some of these questions are: What levels of useful skills have been attained? What areas of learning are to be undertaken? What degree of competence is to be attained? Where is the learning to be done?

When a pupil first enters the high school, it is of crucial importance that his real and complete educational status be ascertained and recorded. This means more than the record of promotion from the previous school grade and his rank among classmates. It means a discovery of the level at which each pupil can perform in the various skills he must use to be successful in high school, in his participation in home and community life, and in the vocation of his choice. It also means a determination of how well informed he is in each of several key areas of general information, such as current events, history, literature, and science.

In a school where individual schedules prevail, the home-room teacher must possess a high degree of sensitivity to the changing needs of each pupil. The teacher must be self-questioning and ask, "Is this pupil exhibiting satisfactory growth, and is he making satisfactory progress in carrying out his schedule?" If the answers are in the negative, and if the reasons are obscure, a full-scale staff conference should be held to explore his difficulties and, if necessary, set up a new schedule for him. This special conference would be conducted by the director of guidance. Participants would include the home-room teacher, any teacher-specialists with whom he has been working in recent months, the member of the guidance staff who knows him best, one or both of the parents, and when appropriate, a representative of the firm where he is securing work experience, his pastor, and in some instances, his doctor, a psychiatrist, or someone from the juvenile section of the police force.

The school's dossier for the pupil must be readily available to members of the conference, and a record of the findings and recommendations must be made before adjournment.

In summary, the individualized program advocated here requires thorough guidance and frequent opportunities for a pupil to pursue at convenient times and places the program of work agreed upon as a result of the guidance process.

Content. Some of the curricular content in the individualized work schedule will be quite similar to that found in class-schedule-dominated high schools, but the differences will be most striking. For instance, work-experience education will consume a substantial portion of time for many pupils. Another difference is that work on problems and projects of real significance to pupils will take precedence over the memorizing of organized information from text books or similar sources.

Perhaps the most important characteristic of curricular content in this school will be the manner in which it is assembled and made available to pupils. Since the pupil is expected to work independently, the content must be in relatively small self-contained units or in major projects. Content in this form has the added value of making it reasonably possible for a pupil whose goals or objectives have changed to have an immediate change in curricular content. This potential responsiveness of content to the changing needs of the individual pupil gives assurance of meaning to, and vitality in, his work. It also provides measurable rewards for those who exercise initiative and practice good work habits. Progress in working out his program to completion is the pupil's own responsibility.

Curricular materials of this type are not new to education. The preparation of "units of work," projects," "problems," and "lessons" is well understood and has been refined through much experience. A supply of such materials can be obtained from many existing sources, but to secure the greatest potential for pupil growth and development, the school staff must be constantly at work in the preparation of new materials and in the revision of those in use.

Units of work as used here refer to carefully prepared outlines that define a somewhat complex but purposeful activity requiring a relatively long time for completion. In these outlines, leads are given indicating the means of accomplishment. Also included are references to related knowledge and activities which will enrich the learner's understanding of the project and sometimes stimulate him to follow new leads.

Ordinarily, projects are undertaken by individuals or small work-groups, less often by a class-sized group.

Lessons may be defined as units of work that are limited in scope and require a relatively short time for completion. They are designed in such a manner that pupils of average or better ability can complete them with a minimum of assistance from the teacher. In many cases such lessons are organized into interrelated series so that a pupil may progress independently through a substantial subject matter area. This type of lesson has been designed for correspondence courses and has been used by such schools and by extension divisions of colleges and universities for many years. With these lessons available, a pupil can work more precisely upon materials for which an immediate need is felt and at a rate commensurate with his ability and with the other demands upon his time.

Other available sources of content materials include periodicals, manuals, forms, brochures, and bulletins suitable to the area of interest and work of each pupil.

Text and reference books would also be used. Their contribution would be to assist pupils with their lessons, projects, and work experience, rather than to provide basic content for a course.

Curricular content for meeting requirements in this type of school must be available in small units or lessons. It must be self-contained so that pupils will be stimulated to proceed on their own. It must be accurate, up-to-date, and presented attractively in order to compete with television, radio, and published information now accessible to most pupils. In short, it must reflect the best known principles of learning development.

Scholarship. Manpower shortages of serious proportions now exist in the fields of science, engineering, teaching, and other professions which require an extended period of scholastic preparation. Furthermore, it is estimated that these shortages will continue for many years even if great improvement occurs in recruitment and in the education of qualified candidates for membership in these professions. In some quarters, there is so much concern about these manpower shortages that high schools are being urged to require more mathematics and science courses and to offer more advanced courses in these subjects.

The inadequacy of these proposals for meeting the situation is apparent to many educators familiar with the high school curriculum. Requiring more pupils to take mathematics and science dilutes the effectiveness of instruction to the more able pupils and to those really interested in these subjects. Since securing able instructors in these subjects is recognized as one of the more important tasks in improving the manpower shortage situation, making the most of those obtained is a paramount consideration. This can be accomplished best by individualizing the pupil's program of work in these areas and by using the science and mathematics instructors as consultants. On this basis, the talented pupils can pursue these subjects at their own pace and often can reach a degree of competence even beyond that deemed necessary for college entrance.

The individualized work program also gives a very great advantage to recruitment of high school pupils into these critical fields of endeavor. High school pupils sometimes become interested in the fields of science and mathematics late in their high school career. In a rigidly class-scheduled type of program, further complicated by an accepted hierarchy of courses, the pupil is advised that it is now too late to take the courses required for college entrance in these fields unless additional time is spent in the high school.

If a pupil possessed the requisite ability for succeeding in these fields, he could develop in a short time the competence required for college entrance. Under an individualized program, as here proposed, this could be accomplished because of immediate and substantial interest, because of additional maturity, and because a specific goal and attainable deadline are provided.

The individualized program approach offers still another advantage for recruitment and sustained interest in these important fields. The unit of work and project basis of learning involves pupils with resource-persons — experts, professionals, specialists — from the community in the fields of mathematics and science. Pupils get to know the scientists and engineers of the community and get a direct view of their importance to the community, state, and nation.

Pupil contacts with successful science practitioners should also have the effect of convincing pupils of the necessity — if success is to be attained — of acquiring competence in mathematics, reading, composition, and other related disciplines as well as in the knowledge and techniques of science itself.

The proper course that the high school should pursue in order to accomplish its highest function — the greatest possible development of the intellect of each pupil — has been, and is now, much debated. Two contrasting points of view are being advocated with relatively equal vehemence. One point of view holds that pupils should be required to do what competent adults have found must be done and to do it in a sequence determined by adults to be logical. This point of view can be implemented quite well in class groups and with a heavy reliance upon text books. An approach such as this appeals to many military authorities and to others who believe the path to improvement of the educational program of the high school is a better mastery of subject matter.

Requirement of pupil mastery of difficult subject matter in a predetermined logical sequence is considered by many to be synonomous with scholarship.

Much of the current literature dealing with high school education and especially with principles of growth, development, and learning of adolescents discredits an emphasis upon "requirements" and upon the validity of many sequential subject-matter patterns as an effective approach to education.

In place of reliance upon "requirements" and "logical" sequences, many educators and psychologists now stress the importance of a felt need by the learner and the presence of some near point value as well as the more remote ones of success in college and in a profession. In the approach which is here proposed, the teaching staff is much concerned with the stimulation of pupil interest, or the early discovery of it in pupils. It is also concerned with pupil involvement in planning what should be done in pursuit of this interest. This pupil interest and participation is guided by the teaching staff into avenues most conducive to pupil growth and development in this and related fields of interest.

This approach assures an understanding by the pupils of the significance of what is being done, and this in turn provides motivation for deep penetration into the field of study and for a study of related fields — both study habits that characterize real scholarship.

There are those who hold that some areas of learning that are of great importance to society will not be undertaken at all if they are permitted to await the felt needs and interests of high school pupils. Philosophy, higher mathematics, and the technical aspects of science are some of the areas about which such persons have this concern. The authors of this book would share this concern if they were not convinced that each pupil, as he pursued his individual goals, would at an early date feel the need for involvement in, and understanding of, such disciplines. It is the responsibility of each staff member to exploit such pupil interest when it occurs.

More specifically, the authors hold that when a pupil has close contact with architects and engineers, he becomes aware that he can not do such work until he masters higher mathematics. Similarly, in his consultations with his teachers and with religious leaders, politicians, members of the various profesions, key figures in industry, labor, and civil service, and in his work-experience education in these fields, he will see philosophies at work and will recognize the necessity for possessing a philosophy if he is to succeed as a leader.

In each of the illustrations mentioned above, the teaching and guidance staff of the school must be ready with the necessary information and materials to expedite the pupil's pursuit of these new-found interests.

Heretofore, the success of the pupil-interest approach to the improvement of high school education has been hampered by the presence of rigid class scheduling and too heavy reliance upon ground covered in text books. Individualized programming of pupils' work as here proposed gives a free hand in the selection of units of work and of study materials. It gives the teacher an unhampered opportunity for stimulating growth and development in terms of the need of each pupil, rather than in terms of the needs of a class or in terms of requirements that all pupils must cover in order to secure credit for the course.

Scholarship potential and achievement are individual matters. A high school educational program, therefore, that is individualized is well adapted for using objective measures of scholarship achievement. It is also an excellent system for exacting from each pupil a standard of excellence appropriate to the individual goals agreed to by the pupils as a basis for formulating their individual programs.

Evaluation. Evaluation, record-keeping, and pupil accounting activities have more than ordinary importance in a high school in which individualized schedules prevail, in which the educational value of off-campus experience is taken into account, and in which growth and development replace accumulation of information as evidence of educational advancement. In this type of high school, it is essential that at all times the staff members have available the kinds of records and evaluations necessary to assist each pupil to move expeditiously from where he is to the attainment of the goals set forth in his schedule of work.

It is therefore necessary to have on file, in usable order, much personal and anecdotal information about each pupil as well as records of his scholastic accomplishments and his scores on many types of standard tests. His abilities, aptitudes, interests, and limitations must be known by the members of the school staff who have responsibility for determining appropriate curricular content for him and for guiding his educational progress.

In the pupil's file, therefore, data would appear in the form of cumulative records on home environment, hobbies, work experience, community and social activities, health, and physical fitness. Some of these data would appear as quantitative records while others would be anecdotal.

It is in order here to identify some of the special demands made upon pupil data in an individualized educational program. These data are used primarily as the basis for staff evaluation of pupils' growth to date in order to guide them more expeditiously into patterns for further development. In this type of program, evaluation and adjustment are almost continuous instead of being merely periodic, as once a year or once a semester.

Much staff time is spent in interviews with pupils rather than in class instruction. Each such interview, to be most helpful, poses the possibility of use in the pupil's data folder and also of the need for making additions to it.

In an individualized program, these records must serve, in a more adequate manner, the purposes traditionally met by term, semester, or course grades.

Instead of a single mark or grade, which inadequately evaluates a pupil's status or performance for a term's work in a subject, the records in a school with individualized scheduling must be more clinical in nature and show evidences of growth and development as well as evidences of current skills, abilities, and competencies in each area of education. It is these records that justify the school's recommendations for college entrance, for work experience, or for employment after school days are over. Adequate records of this type enable the school to perform a really professional task of evaluation of pupils for college entrance or for employment.

The processing, filing, and using of this type of pupil record constitutes a major task of the school. Competent clerical assistance is imperative. The use of microfilm is of great assistance both in use-facilitation, in reduction of filing problems, and in providing the number of copies required for home-room teachers, teacher-specialists, guidance staff, and administrators.

The volume and complexity of pupil records required to do a satisfactory job when individualized schedules are used also makes it necessary to have a key accumulative record card that condenses the data in a pupil's folder as much as possible. This key data card will often expedite pupil interviews and will serve as the permanent record for the pupil when he leaves school.

When an individualized schedule is used, attendance records pose a special problem as compared with recording class attendance. This is brought about partly because of legal requirements for attendance in order to obtain state or federal financial assistance and partly because of the need of documenting pupil time spent on projects, problems, and lessons as one of the bases for evaluation. Although it is more difficult and complex than has been the case in conventional high school record-keeping, the essential time-recording in an individualized school should yield to IBM types of procedures and machine processing. Here again, the importance of supplying adequate clerical assistance to staff members is apparent.

If the individualized high school becomes general, it would not be at all impossible for state financial aid to be based upon enrollment or some type of case-load documentation.

In summary, it should be re-emphasized that the essence of an individualized educational program lies in often repeated evaluations made on the basis of adequate data which are used constantly by staff members in guiding pupils into suitable growth and development activities.

Scheduling. Making suitable arrangements for pupil growth and development and for measuring progress is an Herculean task to be performed by the administration staff of a high school. Such efforts normally result in a schedule of some sort. Generally speaking, a high school schedule identifies the teacher, class group membership, and course name as well as the time, place, and duration of the class period. Sometimes study periods or library periods are similarly scheduled. This arrangement has the obvious and very great advantages of simplifying pupil accounting. His whereabouts under such a system can be determined rapidly at any time during the school day, and the amount of time he spends on each kind of subject matter can easily be documented. This type of scheduling also permits easy control and equalization of the work load of teachers on the basis of time spent in charge of classes.

Even with all of the housekeeping and accounting advantages of class-type scheduling, it has serious shortcomings when it comes to creating a suitable setting for growth and development patterns. The needs, interests, capacities, and rate of learning of many individual pupils become submerged in class control machinery under this type of scheduling. Readiness for the class work of the day may well be lacking in some members of the class. The attention of the entire class often must be given to the teacher's assistance to one pupil, even though it is of no practical interest to the rest of the class. Some would not need such help and others might not be ready for it.

Individualized pupil schedules are proposed as a substitute for class schedules. The proposed schedules deal primarily with a clear definition of what is to be mastered before the school can grant a coveted job or college recommendation and before the school can place a stamp of competence upon a pupil.

Since individual pupil schedules are formulated during the thorough guidance process mentioned above, the schedules, in effect, constitute an agreement between the pupil and the school. These schedules tell the pupil specifically what he must accomplish in order to be prepared to take the next major steps toward his ultimate educational goals. The schedule also clearly sets forth what the pupil must accomplish to obtain school support for job-getting or for college entrance. In addition to clarifying the pupil's working relation with the school, the individualized schedules make it clear to each pupil that he may proceed at his own pace to fulfill the tasks called for in the schedule. This characteristic has great significance in meeting the special educational needs of gifted pupils. No longer will the gifted pupil be subjected to the staleness and boredom which are an inevitable consequence of his being held to the class pace of accomplishment and to the — for him — meager content to which a class group is limited.

The special problems of slow learners are likewise more readily solved if an individualized pupil schedule is used. The rate of progress and the content can both be geared to the ability of each individual. With this type of scheduling, it should be noted that the special problems of both the gifted and the slow pupils can be met without the formation of special classes.

The contents of a pupil's schedule would depend upon a number of factors: educational objective; vocational interests, goals, and employability; previous experiences and accomplishments in and out of school; level of performance in academic skills; health and physical condition; social competence; ability as measured by mental tests; home environment; participation in church and club work, community recreation programs, etc.; recreational interests and activities; and the requirements of state law and school district regulations.

After giving consideration to these and other factors, a pattern of specifics evolves: Just what is to be done and by what means? Where will it be done? When will it be done? What level of accomplishment is required, and by what means and under what conditions will evaluation and testing be done?

The specifications of what is to be done may well include individual lessons for improvement of skills. It may include class work. It may include problems or projects for giving experience in analysis and problem solving. It may specify activities for providing opportunities in the improvement of social competence, group dynamics, or physical-conditioning. It may include work experience on or off campus.

Location of these activities need be specified only when they can best be done away from the home-room. The home-room, with its suitable pupil stations, is designed to make it possible for much of pupil's on-campus work to be done right there. Exceptions would occur when the pupils are working with teacher-specialists, or are exercising for body conditioning. Much of the exercise could be done off-campus at times other than during the normal school day. In these cases, the schedule specifies where, when, and with whom the exercise is to be taken.

When and where activities and work are to be performed should be the pupil's decision unless some restraining factor is involved. If groups are involved and the use of specialized spaces and equipment is required, an imposed time schedule becomes imperative. This should be kept as flexible as possible and changes should be expected as the semester proceeds. Improvement in the productive use of his time should be an important concomitant of the general development of a pupil. This development requires the pupil's management of his own time schedule to the greatest possible extent.

Whenever possible, the pupil's schedule should identify the level of accomplishment to be attained, and the testing and evaluation procedures to be followed in order to determine its attainment.

Individualized scheduling has a distinct advantage over class scheduling for the pupil who is still in search of a permanent goal. For such a pupil, the schedule could be basically exploratory. As a pupil works toward completion of a schedule, his goals may become clearer. At that time, without delay, he can begin on a work schedule in direct pursuit of his new-found goals.

In summary, the individualized schedule is a clearly stated work order for the pupil. It is the pupil's responsibility to complete the work specified. It is the school's responsibility to provide the consultations, assistance, reading materials, space, equipment, and supplies necessary for each pupil to complete his scheduled work. It is also the school's responsibility to evaluate work done by the pupil and to assist him in setting up a new schedule of work.

Staffing. Staff competence, retraining, and assignment are without question the most important factors affecting program improvement. No matter what is done in other aspects of the undertaking, the effort will be of no avail unless there is an appropriate and competent staff devoted to making a success of the enterprise. With such a teaching staff, some success will be attained even though the scheduling and plant provisions are not completely suitable.

Similarly, no matter how good the physical plant is, or how competently the guidance function is performed, the only program improvement that can be accomplished is that of which the staff is capable. Much less than maximum capability can be expected if it is difficult for students to find time to spend with their teachers and counselors or if the physical setting for consultation is not conducive to rapport.

The educational program proposed here would be staffed as in any high school, with administrators, counselors, teachers, and clerical workers. The staffing, however, differs substantially from that of most traditional high schools in duties and responsibilities assigned to teachers, and in the higher ratio of clerical workers to teachers. These differences in duty assignment are better identified as differences in time spent and in emphasis on certain activities rather than differences in the nature of the duties.

In an educational program where individualized work schedules prevail and where growth and development of pupils is of more concern than the mere accumulation of information, teachers perform more as pupil counselors, guides, and consultants than as instructors.

Group instruction, to be sure, has its place but is given only when the need for it appears and in the least amount that will enable the pupils to proceed again independently. Included in such a group would be only those in need of the instruction.

From the point of view of the pupil, the greatest differences between the program proposed here and conventional programs are that under the new approach:

a. He can always, when he so desires, find a place to work alone or with a small group of his peers.
b. When working alone or with a small group, his counselor — the home-room teacher — is ready at hand to help him over difficulties or to refer him to an appropriate teacher-specialist.
c. Teacher-specialists are available for appointments with pupils during the school day by virtue of being free from class instruction duties.
d. Responsibility for having something to do would be his, not the teacher's.
e. He is judged upon ability to perform without reference to how long a time was taken to acquire that ability or where it was acquired.
f. In situations where the pupil's experience is an important consideration, his total experience is taken into account, not merely that occurring at school.
g. Class instruction consumes a minor and irregular part of his school time rather than being dominant.

In order to staff this type of educational program, it is proposed that a home-room teacher be assigned general responsibility for a group of fifty pupils. The assignment of pupils would be made initially by the administrative staff in cooperation with the guidance staff and the home-room teacher group. The home-room teacher and these pupils would normally stay together throughout the pupils' entire high school career. The basic task of the home-room teacher would be to maintain conditions suitable and stimulating for both individual and group work by pupils. He would serve as consultant in group dynamics for his pupils. The special contribution of the home-room teacher in maintaining these conditions is his suitability as a guide and counselor to each pupil in his group. His understanding of the pupils' backgrounds, characteristics, educational goals, and special needs is essential if he is to serve effectively as guide and counselor and to help pupils over difficulties encountered.

In the performance of duties as guide and counselor, he would assist his pupils in finding relevant published materials and would refer them to appropriate teacher-specialists or to community resource-persons who could be of assistance. He would make available to the pupils necessary lesson materials and supplies and would give tests at appropriate times or arrange for teacher-specialists to give them. He would be responsible for keeping necessary records on his pupils' whereabouts during the school day, their progress in working out individual schedules, and their needs for revised or new schedules.

It is proposed that each two home-room teachers have one clerk to assist in the keeping of records, the making of appointments, and the handling of instructional materials. It is also proposed that the home-room teacher be made responsible in his group of fifty for the development of social competence in citizenship, the languages, arts, and communicative skills. In that capacity, he would arrange for class instruction in addition to individual activities in these fields, or work in smaller groups, as conditions warranted.

The home-room teacher would also be responsible for bringing in appropriate resource-persons from among the teacher-specialists or from the community resource group. Contacts between school and home would normally be made through him. One exception to this channeling would be home visits by teacher-specialists for the purpose of observing or evaluating pupil projects being conducted there.

Staffing the proposed school for work in the specialized fields of learning is done by providing an appropriate number of teacher-specialists for each field. These fields of learning include science, mathematics, foreign language, home-making, business education, music, speech arts, arts and crafts, vocational trades and industries, health, and physical education and recreation. These teacher-specialists are primarily resource-persons. They will serve as consultants to pupils and to home-room teachers. Although primarily they will assist pupils in setting-up and carrying to completion projects and units of work in their special fields, from time to time they will give group instruction and demonstrations. Each teacher-specialist within the field of his specialization will have the responsibility of determning for the school the steps of progress made and the degree of competence attained by pupils with whom he works. Each teacher-specialist will have available the special facilities for instruction, projects, consultation, and testing in his field.

It is essential that each teacher-specialist have a studio or clinic-type office appropriate for consultation with individual pupils or with small groups of pupils. It is equally essential that teacher-specialists be available throughout most of the school day for appointments with pupils or with home-room groups when desired by the home-room teachers.

In order to be effective in this type of program and duty assignment, each group of teacher-specialists will need at least one clerk to arrange appointments and to take care of supplying special equipment to be used by pupils.

The number of each type of teacher-specialist that should be provided in an individual school depends upon a number of things, a few of which are listed here: proportion of students for whom high school is terminal formal education; proportion who are college bound; vocational opportunities available in the community; degree to which each community looks to the school for training in home-making, the vocations, or physical fitness; current problems of national security or economy such as are now exemplified by the need for scientists, engineers, and teachers.

Physical Plant. A suitable physical environment has a role so important that the degree of success of an effort toward program improvement is closely related to it. The best efforts of the most competent staff using the best curricular content, applying the best known methods of teaching, guidance, and evaluation, and working in a highly favorable climate of public opinion and acceptance can not achieve success until an appropriate physical plant is provided.

The educational program proposed here requires a physical plant different in several respects from the existing type.

Traditional class scheduling requires that the proper kind of classrooms and other instructional spaces be provided in sufficient number so that all groups can be accommodated.

Individualized pupil scheduling requires different provisions and a different emphasis. It is necessary to provide accommodations for pupils to work on individual problems, projects, units of work, and lessons. Each pupil must be provided with a suitable permanent work station in a setting where individual work may be done effectively, and where needed equipment and materials are easily accessible. This type of pupil scheduling and work also requires that a home-room teacher be readily available and have facilities that permit private consultations. Conference rooms also must be available in spatial arrangement so that work in small groups may be conducted under the supervision of the home-room teacher.

The proposed program also requires that teacher-specialists have studio or clinic-type offices that make it possible to hold conferences with pupils throughout the school day in a setting appropriate to the specialized subject matter involved.

Emphasis in the proposed program upon work-experience education permits the provision of fewer facilities in business education, in the trades and industries, and other vocational programs than is found in a traditional plant. It may also influence the plant provisions for arts and crafts in a similar manner.

In the proposed program the campus needs fewer facilities than are generally provided for physical education and recreation. This is possible because of the use of off-campus facilities either during the school day or at other times. In the proposed program the school has responsibility for assisting pupils in scheduling a suitable daily and weekly program of health maintenance, physical education, and recreation, but not necessarily for executing all of it on campus. Community recreation facilities may be used during or after school hours; so may church, lodge, club, camp, and other types. Privately owned facilities such as bowling alleys, swimming pools, and golf courses may also be used. The proposed program would also affect the type of physical education facilities provided because of the emphasis upon life-long active recreation rather than upon major sports which soon become passive recreation to most people.

The problem of providing adequate corridors for peak periods of pupil traffic is greatly reduced in the proposed program because of the elimination of class periods with a complete change at the close of each period. Conversely, the use of staff members as consultants rather than as class instructors requires intercommunicating facilities equal to the best found in commerce and industry. It also calls for closed-circuit television with outlets throughout the plant.

The educational program proposed here requires a greater amount of building space in some areas than has been provided traditionally. It makes heavy spatial demands for accommodating a great variety of books, pamphlets, and lesson materials in such a manner that they may be assembled and carted to any place on the campus where they are needed. Similarly, the program demands a great variety of work materials, equipment, and models to be used in connection with pupil projects, problems, and lessons. Suitable storage must be provided for these materials. Likewise spaces must be provided for clerks employed to care for them, and to accommodate the carts to transport them.

The proposed program also makes extra spatial demands for clerical workers and record files. An individualized program, and one that takes into full account off-campus work done by pupils, requires much more than the traditional amount of pupil accounting and record-keeping. Such work can not be done by teachers when the demands upon their time are so great for pupil consultation, instruction, and evaluation.

Guidance, curriculum-making, and revision are other services in the proposed program which require more floor space and facilities than are often found in high schools. The entire program would collapse if adequate guidance and curriculum-making services were not provided to assist home-room teachers and pupils in preparing and keeping up-to-date individual pupil work schedules.

There are, of course, a number of facilities in the proposed high school that would be quite comparable to those that are now common. Facilities for vocational agriculture are a case in point. For more than a quarter century, this work has been taught mainly on an individual project basis with off-campus work given due attention and with adequate facilities to implement the program.

Administration quarters would not be substantially different. The same is true of the cafeteria, social rooms, and meeting rooms for demonstrations, little theater, and auditorium purposes.

The physical plant implications of this new educatonal program are discussed above in general terms only. In the following chapter, specific requirements for each part of the plant are given in more complete form.

Facilities Required for the

Program Proposed

In setting down the eductional functions to be housed in various parts of a high school plant, the following points should be borne in mind.

1. The basis for deciding what should be included is severely functional. The criterion used is: What facilities are required to implement generally accepted educational theory? This approach differs from the one that leans heavily upon an evaluation of existing buildings for a determination of what should appear in a proposed school.

The basic importance of this approach is better understood in the light of the great gap that exists between most current high school educational programs and a program that is defensible in terms of the recommendations found in nearly all of the current literature in the secondary education field. Evaluations of existing high school plants too often are made to determine how well they work for a type of program that should be abandoned.

The fact is sometimes overlooked that, in most instances, the facilities in existing buildings are the result of compromises. It is also overlooked at times that building solutions that were good when the building was planned are no longer tenable. The requirements of education have been changing rapidly and will continue to do so. The planning of each new high school building offers a splendid opportunity for exploiting fully the physical requirements of new curricular content, new types of activities and experiences, and new concepts of learning, growth and development.

This opportunity can better be exploited with a completely new and professionally competent analysis of needs than from the selection of "good" parts of existing buildings, which even at best may reflect compromises. Compromises, if found necessary, should be made from an ideal solution, not from a previous compromise.

2. On-campus buildings and facilities should *supplement* those that are already available, or can better be made available, in the community. Education will have more vitality for students, if every opportunity is taken to have it occur in a *real* setting rather than in an artificially created one on a school site. This is of special significance in citizenship training, community education and service, vocational educational work, and sports and recreation, and involves the use of parks and playgrounds, art museums, libraries and other cultural centers.

3. Where conflict in school plant provisions occurs between the requirements of groups or classes and those of individuals, the matter should be resolved in favor of the latter. Instead of determining the capacity of a high school in terms of the class periods that can be scheduled throughout the day, capacity is better determined in terms of being certain that there are a sufficient number of appropriate individual work stations so that each student can be working effectively on his individual program of activities and developmental tasks, except where group work can be just as, or more, efficient in terms of achievement.

4. The teaching staff, except the counselor-teacher-guide (home-room teacher) who is in administrative charge of a group of fifty pupils, is to serve primarily as resource-persons and consultants, and secondarily as group instructors and lecturers.

5. All members of the teaching staff are to be supplied with competent clerical assistance for keeping records and supervising materials. Some of this service is to be done by people on the pay-roll and some by pupils as part of their training.

6. Academic content will not normally appear as textbooks but as relatively small units of work and lessons similar to those done by the better correspondence schools. Teachers can thus pinpoint the satisfaction of the educational needs of individuals as they are determined, and pupils can proceed by themselves at their own rate to satisfy the needs.

Home Room   Home-rooms, which are really housing units for basic student groups, are an absolute essential for the proposed high school. The number of these rooms depends upon the enrollment—one room for each fifty students. With this number in mind, each room is designed and equipped for a capacity of fifty students who remain, when possible, as a group throughout the high school years. The same teacher continues in charge during this entire period and provides the link between pupil and home, and pupil and community.

Although this room is a group room, there is much conferring between the teacher and individual pupils as they work at their assigned stations—home bases.

Not all of the work is individual. A substantial amount of time is spent in small groups and in committee activity. These small groups contain from two to ten students. A lesser amount of time is spent in medium-sized groups of from ten to twenty-five and least with the entire group as a unit.

It is necessary that opportunities be provided for various groups to be working simultaneously. For example, a group of twenty pupils can be busy with one project while other groups are similarly engaged in the conference room or the project workroom.

Arrangements are made for each individual and group to have as much privacy as possible for discussion and work, but at the same time provide visibility for supervision and accessibility for instruction.

Individual activity consists largely of reading, writing, computing, the preparation and assembly of reports and projects. It also involves the use of reference books, pictures, charts, maps, and models. In doing this work, the pupil must be accessible to other pupils, to the teacher, and to specialized staff members. Groups of all sizes are planning together; conferring; working on projects, problems, and reports; receiving instruction; listening to consultants and class members; using audio-visual and other instructional aids and reference works; practicing skills; and assisting each other as needed. Some leave the group temporarily and return with advice and books or materials to further their own or the group's work.

All work stations, both individual and group, within this unit are designed for a great variety of activities, easy mobility of and accessibility to students, and the use of a rich variety of work aids and materials. The entire facility, which is supervised by one teacher, is conceived as a single unit which can, when occasion demands, be subdivided as indicated above. This facility, whenever possible, includes the adjacent outdoor space as part of the work and supervision unit.

One of the available spaces is equipped as a project work area supplied with running water, sturdy water-repellent work surfaces, and ample storage for work materials and equipment. Connection with the out-of-doors is recommended for construction of larger projects.

Another space is designed as a conference room with good acoustics, opportunities for using chalk boards and bulletin boards; opportunities for using and storing maps, charts, and graphs. Tables and portable chairs are provided here.

The home-room teacher's office is designed for private consultation with individual students, faculty specialists, and community resource-persons. It is accessible from the room entrance and provides a complete view of the home-room unit. It is equipped with a teacher's desk, chair, and two side chairs; accommodation for a clerk; ample file cabinets for individual folders containing pupil records and correspondence with community resource-persons and firms; devices readily accessible for reference and for frequent changes of the individual work and progress schedules of pupils; personal professional library; and campus intercommunication to all faculty specialists, the communications center, and the administrative center, as well as telephone connection with the outside.

Since this is the home-room for fifty students for an extended period of time, provision is made in or near the unit for wrap storage, personally owned books, and other personal equipment. Part of this is in the student station and part of it in lockers and cubicles.

Science   The science teacher-specialist has a most important function to perform in the high school today. He develops any spark of scientific interest that has been found by the guidance staff. He is also the key person to develop this interest among pupils who previously were incurious.

Perhaps the most challenging task is to give such direction to the pupil's interest that he will be willing to undertake the high school mathematics necessary for accomplishment in this field. The individual pupil program, in contrast to the class-schedule program, makes an important contribution in the fields of science and mathematics. Under the class-schedule approach, the pupil may not realize the need for mathematics in a science career until it is too late to enroll in the appropriate course. In the individualized program, the pupil pursues his vital interest in science under the guidance of the specialist until he is completely convinced of the need for mathematics, if he is to pursue his science inquiries either in or out of college. Mathematics thus becomes much more than a requirement for college entrance. It becomes a vital and well-understood part of the pupil's growth and development in the field of science.

The science teacher-specialist is prepared to go to home-room groups when requested by the teacher, to interpret science in the news, to help the teacher with the science implications of a group project, or to accompany the home-room group on a visit to an industrial, agricultural, or medical laboratory. He also develops a list of community resource-persons who can be used by the home-room teachers or by himself, on appropriate occasions.

In his headquarters, each science specialist has an office for consultations with individuals and small groups of pupils. Adjoining this, he has a small preparation space, or laboratory. This space is used by the instructor to prepare demonstrations and illustrated lectures; to explain, illustrate, and interpret points in his office consultations; to originate demonstrations for closed circuit television; and to conduct experiments of his own. This room is shared by two or more specialists in a given science area. There is one of these rooms for the physical sciences and one for the life sciences. Convenient to this space is an audio-visual demonstration and lecture room with a seating capacity of about one hundred. This room is used by the specialist in cases where it is not practical or effective for him to go to the home-rooms. Of course, this room is used by all of the science specialists as well as others for demonstrations and projected pictures where more than fifty pupils are to participate, and where superior conditions for picture projection are required.

A science experience laboratory that accommodates thirty-six to forty pupils is readily accessible from the suite of offices used by the specialists. The student stations, provision of utilities, storage facilities, floor space allocations, and room arrangement are designed to accommodate any of the science work offered in the high school. This laboratory accommodates projects and experiments that can not be done satisfactorily in the home-rooms. Assignment of pupils to work either on individual or group tasks is made jointly by a home-room teacher and a specialist. When working in the laboratory, the pupil is under the supervision of a specialist.

The responsibility for general supervision of the laboratory while individuals and small groups are working there is shared by the entire staff of specialists with assistance given by advanced students, or cadet college students in training to become science teachers.

The pupil's written record and report on the project, experiment, or unit of work is approved by both the science specialist and the home-room teacher.

By sharing the responsibility for supervising the laboratory, members of the staff of science specialists increase their availability for pupil conferences and for calls to go to home-rooms to assist the teacher with projects involving science.

Provision is made in the laboratory for at least two semi-private spaces where an individual or small group may, when necessary, leave experimental equipment set up for several days and have it undisturbed by others using the laboratory.

Highly specialized science books, charts, and equipment are stored where they are readily available to the teacher-specialist staff. Equipment and supplies necessary for conducting experiments are stored in the laboratory or in space adjoining it. The science books and equipment to be used in the home-rooms are stored in the service center. Safety and security needs are met for dangerous or valuable materials and equipment.

Opportunities for presenting displays are a prominent feature of the science quarters.

The function of the teacher-specialist in mathematics on the high school staff is: **Mathematics**

1. To serve as consultant to home-room teachers and to the home-room groups when they are working on projects having mathematical implications;
2. To serve as consultant and instructor for pupils doing advanced work or who are assisting home-room teachers;

3. To have available for exhibition, demonstration, and use:
    a. the computing and control instruments and devices used in engineering, industry, and business,
    b. complete and cut-away models of complex geometric shapes,
    c. illustrations of tables, graphs, and charts used in reporting quantitative data and relationships,
    d. highly specialized books and other printed materials in the field of mathematics;
4. To assist in curriculum-making, testing, and evaluation.

In serving as consultant to home-room teachers and groups, the specialists assist the students in understanding and interpreting the quantitative portions of data being studied, in making the computations required in the preparation of a report, and in developing methods of presenting data for reports on projects or problems. Some of this consultation takes place in the home-rooms. At other times, home-room teachers, pupils, and pupil committees go to the office of the specialist.

In his work with pupils who are doing advanced mathematics, the teacher-specialist assigns units of work, gives "warm-up" individual or group instruction, is available for consultation when needed, checks upon and evaluates the work done, and certifies to the level of accomplishment attained by the pupils.

A small work-room with a capacity of about fifteen pupil work stations adjoins and is visible from the suite of mathematics offices. This is used by advanced students during the time they are doing work that requires frequent consultation with the specialist.

Inasmuch as science is dependent to a considerable degree upon mathematics, it is desirable to have the offices for these two subject-specialists integrated.

Business Education Teacher-specialists in business education are available for lesson making, instructing, consulting, and testing in typewriting, bookkeeping, shorthand, general business, business machines, office practice, distribution and similar fields. Work in business education traditionally done almost entirely in on-campus business education quarters is performed in several places on and off the campus under the new program. When working alone or in small groups, the home-room is the natural place for such activity. Much office practice, some typing, shorthand, and machine operation are carried out in school offices and for business and professional firms throughout the community. The opportunity for pupils to do such work is dependent upon the possession of specified levels of competence. The specialists are equipped to make such determinations and to cooperate with the guidance staff in an effort to make each pupil's work experience education as rewarding as possible, both for the pupil and for his employer.

Consultation with pupils on the work experience aspects of the total business education program is a major activity of the teacher-specialist. Much work is done on the basis of individual lessons and projects. Some shorthand is practiced from dictating machines. Since home-rooms are equipped with typewriters and read-back machines, much of the time needed to master business techniques is done in these rooms. Distributive educational practice is best done in cooperation with business firms in the community.

In addition to one private office for each teacher-specialist, the business suite provides:

1. One typing instruction and practice room—capacity fifty.
2. One business machine laboratory and workroom.
3. One small instruction and pupil workroom—capacity about fifteen—used for small group instruction when occasion demands and for individual work stations for pupils during the time their work requires frequent consultation with a specialist. It is also a meeting place for committees of business leaders and their personnel officers who are advisors to the business education specialist.
4. Storage space for specialized books, pamphlets, periodicals, and testing materials in the field of business. These are in, or adjoining, the suite of offices.
5. Display and bulletin board space.
6. Shelving and cabinets appropriate for storage of paper and business forms in each of the instruction and work rooms.
7. Work bench and running water.

Foreign Languages

The teacher-specialists in foreign languages are engaged in a variety of activities for furthering pupil interest in language study, for increasing skill in language use, and for evaluating progress and accomplishment. These specialists are available as consultants to the home-room teacher, to individual pupils, and to pupil committees. Foreign language clubs look to them for advice and assistance.

The specialists are responsible for the production or acquisition of suitable individual lesson materials and for the selection of phonograph records and other audio-visual aids such as recording equipment.

Each specialist needs a separate office for consultation with pupils. The office is equipped to make and read back voice recordings for pupils, and to record teaching materials that are to be presented in this manner.

Storage space for special language books and periodicals is accessible to the specialists' offices, as are a group of recording and read-back cubicles and a small pupil instruction room with a capacity of about fifteen pupil work stations.

The teacher-specialists use closed-circuit television to some extent in giving instruction.

Speech Arts The speech arts teacher-specialist assists the home-room teachers with oral English—story-telling, expression, public speaking, dramatic skits, and role-playing. He has direct responsibility for school-wide dramatic productions including stagecraft, debates, speech contests, and the like. He also has a close working relationship with some of the communications-center staff in the preparation and production of public relations materials.

The office of one of the speech arts teacher-specialists adjoins the little theater stage. A stagecraft teacher-specialist has his office next to the stagecraft shop which adjoins the stage and is supplied with hand tools, paint, fabric, and lumber.

The little theater and the stagecraft shop is in accord with good practice now found in high schools. The little theater is in the general area of the auditorium, if one is included, but not so close that noise conflicts occur when the two places are in use simultaneously.

If no auditorium is provided, the little theater stage should be of generous size. Seating, if possible, should be appropriate for use by pupils when taking written tests.

Music A school operated predominantly upon the basis of individual pupil schedules creates opportunities for developing a school music program somewhat different from that usually found in schools operated on class schedules.

In current class scheduling practice, it is difficult to separate instruction, which is basically individual in nature, from group performance at school and community functions. When individual instead of class scheduling predominates, it is possible to select apt pupils from the entire student body to compose performance groups. This procedure also makes it possible to involve the talented pupils who are taking private lessons.

An obvious advantage of this arrangement is that talented and advanced students need not enroll in a regular music class in order to participate in school-sponsored group performances, or, in some instances, to acquire an easy unit of credit. When a class is composed of pupils having great differences in ability, the more advanced ones lose much time while the instructor is giving special attention to the beginners. By the same token, when the class work is suited to advanced pupils, the others are, to some extent, marking time.

A pupil may well have any one of three or more reasons for taking music in school. The most common reasons are to increase proficiency in voice or in playing some instrument, to increase competence as a member of a music group, or for recreation.

Effective use of facilities, of staff time, and of pupils' time requires that the first purpose be accomplished largely upon an individual basis and the other two upon temporary grouping and re-grouping bases rather than on a continuing class-group basis. Much of the group performance, as in the case of individual instruction, is done off campus. Group music is performed in churches, club rooms, recreation halls, banquet rooms, residences, and so forth.

The music specialist on the school staff is available to assist the home-room teacher in making out individual schedules for pupils who plan to do some work in music. He is available upon call to go to home-room situations in cases where his expert assistance is needed. He assists the staff in the preparation and revision of curricular materials. He counsels pupils and pupil committees who come to him for help. He gives individual and group instruction in music, instructs apt pupils in the leading of groups in music and, on occasion, leads music groups for the school or for functions where school group music is used.

Facilities for music teacher-specialists include:

1. A studio office for each staff member for consultation and for incidental instruction of individuals and small groups, for library, and for control of closed circuit television.
2. A bank of small practice rooms varying in size to accommodate one to five pupils. Each room is connected with closed circuit television controlled in the specialists' offices. The teacher can cut into the practice room for observation and comment, or the pupil can contact the teacher with request for help.
3. Storage suitable for the checking of privately owned instruments.
4. Storage of school owned uniforms and instruments.
5. Repair bench for musical instruments.
6. A group practice room for all kinds of music. This room takes care of all situations when a suitable room is not available elsewhere on the campus or in the community.

With a high school music program that is closely related to the musical activities of youth in the entire community, it is expected that much practice and performance will take place in facilities other than those of the school.

In a high school where the school, the home, and the community are working closely together to enrich the growth and development opportunities of youth, the homemaking teacher-specialist comes close to being an indispensable resource-person to the home-room teachers. There are many problems and projects upon which pupils are working that have homemaking implications, and in some instances, the project is, in fact, a homemaking project. Furthermore, the specialist, from time to time, needs specialized equipment and the type of materials and supplies that

Homemaking

can not very well be had in connection with a home-room. The specialist also has a key responsibility in connection with work experience education in the categories of home nursing, baby-sitting, and domestic service. This responsibility encompasses selection and training of pupils, and development of programs of school work and study that improve the ability of pupils to render these services. The teacher-specialist also is concerned with giving special instruction and training to those pupils who exhibit a more than average interest and talent in homemaking work, to the end that they can help the home-room teacher and younger pupils with problems. This will enrich their training, looking toward collegiate work in the field of homemaking.

To accomplish these things, the teacher-specialist:

1. Demonstrates on the closed circuit television.
2. Lectures with materials and equipment carted in from the communications center to the home-rooms.
3. Consults with individuals or small groups in his office.
4. Supervises special pupils working in the homemaking laboratory.
5. Goes to pupils' home where projects are being undertaken.

Pupils' clubs with a strong component in the homemaking field also make heavy demands upon the time, skills, and talents of the specialists. Future Homemakers of America, 4H Girls, Campfire Girls, Girl Scouts, are but a few of the clubs with a strong homemaking bent.

Facilities required are:

1. An office suitable for consultations for each of the specialists.
2. A room suitable for club meetings and conferences—capacity about 20.
3. Facilities for making demonstrations in the laboratory and for the closed circuit television.
4. A general purpose homemaking laboratory—capacity 30.
5. Ample display space.

Affinities include art, the industrial arts and crafts.

Arts & Crafts Teacher-specialists in arts and crafts are a most valuable resource to the home-room teacher, to homemaking specialists, to individual pupils, and to clubs, committees, and small groups of pupils working on projects that involve illustration and handwork skills. Some entire projects will no doubt grow out of pupils' contacts with these teacher-specialists.

The art teacher-specialist is in great demand for his technical assistance to pupils who are designing posters for student body elections and student activities.

Another demand on the teacher-specialists' time is serving as advisors to the clubs that are always so popular with pupils of high school age.

Through cooperation with the staff of the communications center and by other means, the arts and crafts specialists are made aware of numerous opportunities for involving pupils in community projects, contests, and other creative activities that require certain interests and skills. The specialists not only assist in getting pupils included in such activities, but help them in securing the greatest educational benefit from such involvement. They then evaluate the individual student's progress.

Out of these contacts with pupils, teacher-specialists find evidence of interest and talent. Such pupil interest and talent is then developed by arranging for more time to be spent by pupils in the development of special skills essential to creative expression. This extra time can be spent with the specialists in doing appropriate work in some commercial or industrial establishment, or in doing work for the school as helpers to the specialists, to the home-room teacher, or in the school's communication center.

The arts and crafts teacher-specialists concern themselves primarily with stimulating pupils' use of creative expression in solving their home, school, and community problems; and in evaluating their progress and proficiency in this field.

Each teacher-specialist requires:

1. A studio office for consultation purposes. The suite of offices is served by
2. A storeroom for special supplies, materials, and equipment.
3. A workroom with a capacity of fifteen or twenty student stations for pupils who are doing work that requires frequent consultation with the specialists. This room also serves as the meeting place for art clubs.
4. Space for a clerical worker to serve the staff of specialists.
5. Liberal amounts of tack and display area.
6. A kiln.

The more important affinities are with the communications center; the homemaking, dramatic, industrial and vocational arts; and recreation specialists.

Industrial and Vocational Arts

Education in industrial and vocational arts—the development of basic tool skills and employability in industry—is occurring throughout the entire school for much of the school time.

The home-rooms are equipped and used for many types of construction projects requiring the use of tools. Home-room teachers need the assistance of industrial and vocational arts specialists in planning and supervising such projects. These specialists also frequently respond to calls for help from the teacher-specialists in dramatics, science, mathematics, home-making, and arts and crafts. Many pupils also need specialists' help on projects which they are doing at home on a do-it-yourself basis or in connection with employment or apprenticeship training that involve the use of tools.

It is emphasized that much of the pupil's work in the fields of trades and industries is done off campus. In that connection there has already accumulated a rich backlog of experience in apprenticeship training and work experience education. This approach is continued and expanded. Craft advisory committees for apprenticeship training illustrate effective involvement of employers in the educational program.

Teacher-specialists have the important task of identifying pupils' capacities for doing jobs in these fields, and more importantly, of providing avenues for increased pupil competence. Where native ability justifies it they help pupils to move into engineering, supervising, and management aspects of trades and industries.

These teacher-specialists are responsible, with the assistance of other staff personnel, for developing projects and for approving those proposed by pupils and others. In the work experience educational program, they confer with the guidance staff to determine the educational value of jobs. They advise pupils and home-room teachers concerning the most helpful related subjects. Generally speaking, pupils' work on the related subjects is done in the home-rooms, but the lesson and work-book materials are those prepared or approved by the specialists.

Since most of the pupils who are headed for trade and industry occupations will be doing work-experience education, there is not the on-campus demand for heavy equipment shops that have been provided traditionally as a part of the school plant. Some kinds of machines, differing according to community and regional industrial emphasis, are provided for instruction and practice. Also opportunities for developing some skills such as welding are provided.

The agricultural program as now found in high schools illustrates best what can be accomplished in an individualized educational program which is built around problems and projects that have real meaning for pupils. The involvement of parents in setting up and approving the projects, of bankers and others in financing them, and of the Grange and Farm Bureau in general sponsorship also illustrates well the concept of using home and community as an educational resource. Furthermore, the teachers in this field have operated largely as consultants to pupils in the conduct of their projects and in the operation of the organization "Future Farmers of America" and "Four-H Clubs."

The high school agricultural program is closely integrated with that of the life sciences. In addition to the generally accepted vocational agricultural program, provisions are made for gardening, landscaping, care of estates and parks, industrial and service activities related to agriculture, such as farm machinery, pest controls, and fertilizers.

Facilities required include an office equipped for consultation, combination library and conference room, agricultural laboratory, and some site area suitable for plant-growing by pupils who do not have home opportunities for such projects.

Each teacher-specialist has an office for consultation and these offices are served by a conference room in which the craft and industry advisory committees meet with the teacher-specialist staff. This conference room also serves as a meeting place for officers and committees of pupils' clubs and organizations in the field of trades and industries.

The offices have ample provision for storage of books and pamphlets as well as for hand tools, gauges, and devices for measuring fine tolerances. Display space for pupils' work is also an essential.

In addition to the agricultural shop, the following specialized shops are provided: wood shop, metal shop, auto shop, electrical shop, and drafting room. Each of these spaces is designed and equipped to give group instruction to beginners in these fields, and also to serve the needs of individuals for improving skills and for meeting special situations which arise in the course of the work-experience education or apprenticeship-training program.

In addition to the various shops, a shop yard, a classroom, and a specialized library, pamphlet, and periodical room are provided for general use by pupils.

The physical education and recreation programs are individualized as they are elsewhere in the school. Responsibility for health examinations, counseling, and physical education is shared with other staff members and off-campus resource-persons. The kinds of health examinations, guidance, and service for which the school takes responsibility are carried out at the center for guidance in cooperation with the home-room teachers. Health education is the responsibility of many staff members including the home-room teachers and the science staff, as well as the physical education staff and any medical or nursing personnel employed by the school. Much in the way of health education resource is available outside the school. Medical and dental associations, as well as individuals in those professions, are generally willing to participate in school health educational programs.

Physical education and active recreation facilities are selected and designed to care for education programs in physical fitness, posture improvement and other corrective exercises, sports, games, and active recreational pursuits, and to accommodate the staff needed to conduct such programs.

Specialized office facilities permit staff members to serve as consultants

Physical Education and Active Recreation

63

in establishing an individualized program for each pupil, to give instruction when needed, and to counsel and advise pupils who have special problems in this field or who exhibit a vocational interest in physical education and recreation.

Since in many communities non-school facilities are available in these fields, the specific items that are to be provided at the school can not be known until the off-campus resources are listed, described, and evaluated for potential usefulness and availability.

The highest priority category of facilities for pupil use are those adapted to remedial and corrective work, including special programs for the physically handicapped. Instruction in this type of program is, of necessity, individual in nature and therefore groups must be small. Twenty would be a maximum number for the more severely handicapped. In less handicapped groups, working in coordinated body movement and posture, twenty-five or thirty is considered a maximum.

Next in priority are facilities that are required for instruction and pupil participation in the type of games and activities which may be expected to be continued in adult life. Among these are a swimming pool, tennis courts, golf (putting green and driving range), archery range, croquet and horseshoe courts, softball fields, volleyball courts, shuffleboard and outdoor bowling layouts, floors for social and square dancing (these may be carried on in multi-use rooms located elsewhere on the campus), paddle-tennis tables, badminton courts, spaces for roller skating, and fly-casting. An instructor may handle as many as forty pupils in most of these activities.

In accomplishing the aims of the high schools the interscholastic sports program must be ranked below the corrective programs and the intramural sports and active recreation programs which pupils enjoy now and will continue to enjoy for many years as active participants. Nevertheless, it is highly desirable that opportunities be given high school pupils for participation in interscholastic basketball, baseball, football, track programs, and tumbling and stunt activities, where health permits and where the time consumed does not penalize the pupil in attaining the over-all objectives established in his individual schedule.

In the design of facilities, the following needs are met:

1. Pupil counseling and individual instruction in performance and safety.
2. Group instruction in performance and safety by staff and by pupils with a vocational interest.
3. Practice activity by individuals or by student groups with minimum of staff participation.
4. Daily exercise and recreation for those whose needs in this category are not met better off campus.

5. Competition in games and sports when not provided adequately elsewhere in the community.
6. Storage and issuance of supplies and equipment, and repairs and protection against damage and theft.
7. First aid service and emergency resting for pupils.
8. Shower, locker, dressing rooms and toilets for pupils and staff.
9. Night use of facilities designed for basketball, tennis, soft ball and table games.
10. Summer use of physical education buildings, pools, courts and fields.
11. Landscaped area for outdoor classroom use, as well as parties and barbecues.
12. Feeding facilities for serving the school.

In designing the facilities for meeting the needs listed above, consideration is given to the following characteristics and requirements:

1. Physical education staff offices are in one suite for both men and women. Each office is useful for private consultation with pupils and faculty members. Staff showers, lockers, and dressing rooms are grouped one each for men and women. The office suite is located between the remainder of the campus buildings and physical education buildings but adjoins one of the physical education buildings.
2. Facilities for group instruction, except as noted for the handicapped, accommodate forty pupils. The acoustical problem of pupil instruction is met either with room conditioning or voice amplification, or both. Where there is a conflict between the physical requirements for instruction and the requirements for competitive or stunt activities, the conflict is resolved in favor of instruction. For example, an even-depth pool takes precedence over a graduated-depth pool with diving facilities at one end. Also the typical gymnasium arrangement in which the recommended basketball court width and a maximum bleacher capacity dictates dimensions is, if necessary, modified in favor of dimensions that facilitate the overlay of sufficient volleyball or badminton courts or other areas to accommodate a group of forty. In designing and locating facilities for instruction, it is assumed that student assistants are available to supplement the instructor's efforts.
3. Insofar as possible, facilities are located and arranged with informal use by pupils in mind. Individuals and small self-formed groups want to practice certain movements and skills when their schedules permit.
4. Some of the pupils are primarily concerned with opportunities for daily exercise either as a supplement to instruction or sometimes in lieu of it. Arrangements are made for use of tennis, badminton, volleyball, and horseshoe courts; table tennis and croquet before and after

regular school hours and during the lunch period. These facilities are designed and located to encourage this type of use.

5. Physical education facilities for sports competition, when justified, follow the traditional pattern in the design of the gymnasium and the stadium.

6. A physical education and active recreation program based upon individual needs and interests instead of primarily upon competitive sports requires a much greater variety and amount of equipment. The space and arrangement required for storing, protecting, repairing, distributing, and collecting this equipment therefore becomes an important factor in the successful operation of the program.

7. As has already been indicated, the provision and control of the·health and resting services for the school is a function of the guidance center. It is necessary, however, to have as a part of the physical education facilities some provision for first aid and for resting.

8. A small individual locker is provided for each pupil enrolled in the school, and a number of larger lockers for street clothes equal to one-fifth of the enrollment. Shower heads are supplied for one-fifth of the enrollment in a ratio of one to each three pupils.

9. Installations for accommodating night use of facilities by pupils and adults include good lighting and ample, well-located auto parking. Facilities most likely to be used are, when possible, grouped together for supervision and custodial care. Some facilities need to be locked off from night use.

10. The design and arrangement of all facilities contemplate practically year-round use. Here again the major considerations are the grouping of those most likely to be used in the summer and the provision of ample, well-located auto parking.

11. A facility that makes a substantial contribution to the blending of school and community, of adolescents and adults, of individuals and families, is a landscaped area that is suitable for barbecues, outdoor parties, and outdoor classroom work for both pupils and adults in the community.

12. The cafeteria facility has importance in areas other than feeding and nutrition. It also serves a useful community purpose in providing meals for social events, banquets, luncheon groups, committee meetings, music practice groups, and recreation events. The dining space, therefore, is designed for use as a large room or a number of smaller spaces.

The service area emphasizes snack bar and lunch counter service for meeting the needs of an informal program with a de-emphasis upon scheduled class periods. The service line is de-emphasized as much as possible by using cart service centers in the dining room and also cart service to the home-rooms when that is desired by home-room groups.

The cafeteria contemplates year-round operation in order to care for summer recreational activities and pupil and adult educational projects that carry through the summer. This consideration locates the cafeteria close to the recreational facilities.

A communications, production, and materials service center is essential in this school. Such a service center becomes imperative when rigid scheduling and classwork domination are replaced with individual scheduling, flexible grouping, and staff and community resource-person approaches. The unit combines in one center the best facilities and practices in intercommunicating devices, in audio-visual services, curriculum laboratory and production practices, and instructional materials center. Whatever printing is done on-campus is done here. The center also serves as headquarters for student body publications. The library services are a functioning part of this unit. The service center houses production experts in curriculum materials, in journalism and public relations, and in programming for and producing of educational television and film materials. This requires a studio office for an illustrator, an office for a curriculum and test materials writer, and an office for a public relations officer. **Communications, Production, and Materials Center**

Teachers' work rooms and conference rooms for curriculum making and revision, as well as for testing and evaluating materials, are a part of the unit. Preparation and control of materials to be distributed to home-rooms or special rooms through tape recordings, radio, or closed television circuits are centered in this unit.

Maintenance of audio-visual equipment, film, and aids is handled here as is the storage of such equipment and materials that can not better be housed in the home-rooms.

In brief, the service center accommodates all staff members who are working on curricular materials and other instructional aids. It also is the principal resource center used by home-room teachers in aiding individual pupils and small groups to work effectively on their programs. Space is provided for accommodating roll-around carts and the activity of assembling and disassembling cart loads of books and materials that are to go to rooms as needed. Another function of the center is to assemble and prepare audio-visual materials which can be "piped" into home-rooms or other rooms upon request. This replaces much of the picture projection within the room.

A substantial portion of the supply-clerk type of work needed in this unit is done by students either in connection with an educational project or as part-time employment or short term full-time employment.

The library renders its traditional services of acquiring, classifying, **The Library** repairing, storing, making available, and checking out and in, the books and other published materials needed by the high school students, faculty, and community personnel who are cooperating with the school. It also gives group demonstrations and lectures on how to use library facilities and services. The traditional services, however, are modified and conditioned by the following: Many books are used over extended periods of time in the home-rooms, in the studios and laboratories housing staff specialists, in the service center, and in the guidance suite. The library staff also, from time to time, needs to go to group rooms to assist with problems and projects. Book carts with suitable storage are needed as a means of getting book assemblies to and from group rooms throughout the plant. Reading room space is provided for ten per cent of the enrollment.

For the library to render maximum service in this type of high school, it is essential that its work be fully and functionally coordinated with the guidance, audio-visual aids, instructional, communicating, and materiel and faculty group services furnished by the school. This requires that the school principal, or a vice principal, be responsible for such coordination of effort. It also requires that the book cart service mentioned above be located near the instructional materials center and near the staff quarters where curriculum construction and revision occur. In addition, there are a few alcove-like rooms which are scheduled for specified periods for older students, for students working on projects the success of which depends upon proximity to library services.

While many books are located for extended periods of time in group rooms about the plant, their control and accounting is still the responsibility of the library.

The library is designed with the idea that much part-time student help will be used both for work-experience education and for part-time employment.

Guidance Center   An expertly-staffed guidance center is indispensable in a school where individual programs of work take precedence over class attendance. The size of such staff depends upon the amount of effective guidance that can be done by the home-room teachers. Even though guidance activity is to be stressed in home-room situations, yet it is essential that guidance specialists be available as consultants to the home-room teachers, to faculty committees on curriculum and evaluation, and to students referred to them by the home-room teachers.

The guidance staff is directly responsible to a director who in turn is responsible to the school principal for coordinating and scheduling the services of his staff. Specialization within the staff provides at least one psychometrist, one occupational information specialist, one boys' counselor, one girls' counselor, and a public health nurse or other medical specialist.

68

This group of specialists represents the board of education and the school administration in carrying out school policy in regard to school-community contacts that are part of the learning experiences of pupils. This includes unpaid and paid pupil employment.

Policies for the programs of community service and campus development projects are carried out through the home-room teachers and the teacher-specialists, but the center is the clearing house for the entire school.

Physical requirements include offices for private conferences with pupils, teachers, and community resource-persons; storage for professional library available to all of the guidance staff and for duplicates of individual pupil folders; a case conference room; waiting-space for pupils; inter-communication connection with all home-room teachers and the administration; and outside telephones. The pupil waiting space is in charge of an especially competent secretary who routes pupils to the appropriate staff member and who supplies proper information when that satisfies the pupil's need. This space is made useful for other purposes so that a pupil who enters is not identified as being in trouble.

Staff offices are designed so that highly technical individual tests may be given here. This requires a typical student station plus adequate storage for specialized test materials.

Of key importance to the effective operation of the guidance center is the provision of a suitable case conference room. This is convenient to the office of the director and the pupil record files and accommodates nine or ten persons including the faculty member making the referral, the home-room teacher concerned, the guidance staff member who knows the pupil best, staff specialists familiar with the work of the pupil, sometimes the nurse, and sometimes the doctor, psychiatrist, or religious leader who has had dealings with the pupil. In addition to conference table seating, the room is equipped with a dictating machine so that a record may be made at once of the conference findings.

The guidance staff must work closely with the staff preparing the content and material for learning experiences, and that responsible for selecting community and school resources for use by the school. This indicates the desirability of locating the guidance center close to the service center and also to the administration.

The administration staff of the high school is headed by a principal. His chief assistants are: **Administration**

1. A vice principal in charge of student affairs, including student body funds, recreation, and plant maintenance.
2. A director of curriculum and instruction who is in charge of the educational program as carried on by the home-room teachers and teacher-specialists on and off the campus. Curriculum making and

modification as well as general control of the service center is also a responsibility of this director.

3. A director of guidance and health services.
4. A director of information and public relations.

The director of guidance is housed in the guidance center, but the rest of the administration staff is housed in its own center close by. In this center are found quarters for the student body government as well as for the administrative staff of the school and its secretarial and clerical personnel.

The secretarial group is housed in one room which includes reception, filing, and storage space for all of the staff but not for the student body offices. The group of offices also is served by a single staff conference room most readily accessible to the principal and the vice principal. Conferences called by the director of instruction and curriculum and by the director of public relations are most likely to be held in the service center.

The principal, vice principal, director of instruction and curriculum, and the director of public relations each has a separate office. Adjoining the office of the vice principal are quarters for a bursar and a bookkeeper. The head custodian, who is also under the supervision of the vice principal, is probably better located at another part of the plant.

Student body quarters consist of a room containing desks and files for a student body president, vice president, and treasurer. The treasurer has a teller's window that opens into the corridor as a reception space. A room that can be used for student council meetings is available close by.

The Educational Plant

7

Up to this point we have concerned ourselves with educational programs. We have examined the strength and weakness of current policy and practice and have come up with a proposal which we believe provides an answer to one of the weakest points in the educational offering currently found in America: that is, its lack of recognition of the individual. And we have outlined the general and specific principles of school plant design that would best serve a high school which emphasizes the individual development of the pupil.

Having formulated the educational program and its plant requirements, it is next in order to examine an actual proposed school plant design.

We are somewhat apprehensive about offering building plans lest they be regarded as the final and only answer to the requirements of the educational program; the appearance of plans in a book often invests them with an authority we do not intend. Scores of different building plans may be designed which meet the specifications equally well. There may be variations which come from different sites and climates, as well as different arrangements of buildings and rooms. But since a plant plan is necessary to complete this study in education, we offer this one. No doubt you will do it differently and better; please do.

A temperate climate and a fairly level site were chosen. This site, including the buildings, gardens, game fields, and parking areas occupies approximately fifty acres. It is bounded on the north by a river and on the west by a main vehicular artery which connects it to the adjoining residential areas and the business and industrial sections of the community. To the east and south are other residential areas. Green strips extend into these adjoining residential sections, providing pedestrian access to the school and supplementary game and recreation areas, to be used jointly by the school and the community. Because of the dependence of the educational program on the resources of the community, convenience of access—both vehicular and pedestrian—is necessary. Ample parking areas for vehicles are provided for both students and public. Every consideration is given to public use since the school offers both adult education classes and facilities such as the auditorium and the swimming pools which will be used frequently by the members of the community. In addition, the school depends on the personal contribution of time and effort by citizens for teaching and consultation services.

The entire plant is enhanced by a park-like setting with gardens. This is necessary, if the school is to provide the best that the community can offer as a focal point for its life as well as a beautiful environment in which its future citizens are to learn and to grow. With some exceptions most of America's schools, either because of cost limitations or because of a fear that pleasant surroundings represent educational frills, fail to provide a setting such as the one visualized here.

The temperate climate assumed for this location has led to the use of roofed, but open-air, corridors for pedestrian traffic. Outdoor swimming pools, game courts and playfields, and an outdoor theater, as well as the use of open-air courts for educational purposes, have proved feasible in climates such as the one chosen for this project. Increased weather protection and changed building arrangements are recognized as necessary for other climates.

There are many vast urban secondary schools with large enrollments whose institutional mien is oppressive and in whose cavernous interiors little recognition is granted to the students' individuality. Experience with such schools has given educators a commendable desire to provide educational buildings and surroundings which are friendly and where the young student finds an atmosphere which allows him to develop his individual characteristics and interest. This school center houses approximately 1200 young people. In this building complex are provided spaces and facilities covering a complete range of physical and mental interests. It is a large building group. The building units are closely joined and some of the units cover large areas of interior space. Before considering the reasons for this, a word is offered here in explanation of the large-building concept. Twelve hundred students exploring the whole range of human interests require large areas and large buildings. These are scaled down to the individual, with spaces and equipment assigned to these individuals, and with other building features such as the commons room, the dining facilities and the open-air courts which encourage the development of friendships, and which dignify such enjoyments and activities as eating and playing games. A large building group invites the unfavorable cry "institution." An institution can be friendly and it is hoped that this one is.

Even in an educational program which has been thoughtfully formulated,

72

conditions change in a changing world. For this reason flexibility of many kinds has been sought. The home-room building units, each of which houses approximately 300 students, have been grouped closely together. This permits the easy shifting and re-grouping of age groups which constantly fluctuate. This also permits the closer correlation of the work between different age groups. Each one of the home-room building units is expected to house the ninth, tenth, eleventh and twelfth years. A group of students may remain in the same home-room unit for four years or may be shifted each year. Complete flexibility of partitions and equipment is provided in all of the home-room units as well as in all other buildings of the entire plant.

The loft type of educational area is a characteristic of this school plant.

Separate buildings of the school plant are designed to include within their perimeter walls related learning experiences among which affinities exist. Although affinities exist among all fields of experience and knowledge, a desire to limit building areas to manageable dimensions led to a grouping of fields of study that were most closely related.

When education dictated by class schedules is discarded, and the individual is encouraged to study and learn in accordance with his own needs, then a school plant must function to place within easy reach of the individual student all of the teachers, specialists, and resources of the entire plant. Room arrangements are planned to accomplish this.

Space relationships become more complex than in a schedule-dominated school plant. Distance is measured in terms of resistance to the development of an idea by means of reference, consultation, and discussion, and can no longer be measured in terms of the time it requires to change classes. A loft type of plan seems to permit the closest relationship between the individual parts of a large complex of laboratories, offices, and consultation rooms. This is illustrated most forcefully by the building for Specialized Learnings; the building which houses the Communication and Materials Center, the Administrative Offices, the Guidance Center, and the Library, as well as the home-room building units achieve flexibility in the same way.

The loft type of plan results in a building which is characteristically a large space tending to a square in shape, obstructed as little as possible by structural or supporting elements or mechanical equipment. The squarish shape and the needed dimensions result in an area of such magnitude that a satisfactory lighting environment cannot be contrived by means of windows alone. Top lighting, either natural or artificial, is an inevitable consequence. Windows can not provide enough ventilation, and a system of mechanical ventilation is another inevitable characteristic of the loft plan.

There is usually a portion of the space at the center of a loft plan area which is removed a distance from the outside wall so that the likelihood of obtaining a view of the outside is remote. Views of the natural outside surroundings of buildings are desirable. But if contact by all internal spaces with an outside wall can be secured only at a sacrifice of the effectiveness of the educational operation, then a choice must be made.

The experience of the authors provides a conviction that interior areas can be pleasant and stimulating. Perhaps the belief of most of us, that a view of the outside is a fundamental human requirement, may be instead a habit acquired through centuries of custom and experience. We are not saying, however, that interior areas without views are suitable for daily periods of long sustained work. The normal experience of any user of this school plant exposes him to contact with a variety of rooms, some with entirely interior walls, some with an exterior window wall.

The loft plan can permit a high degree of flexibility in the location and movement of partitions; there is great opportunity to construct rooms of any size or proportion with a maximum of choices in solving complex problems of space assignment and relationships. Thus the loft plan permits the architect freedom for planning spaces, and later offers the educator an equally wide opportunity for adapting his school plant to changed requirements and uses. This flexibility reverses the traditional domination of the educational program by the confines of the walls and allows instead the needs of the program—no matter how it may change—to determine the shape of the space needed.

Importance is attached to any medium of communication in direct proportion to its contribution to the learning activity. Books are always important to learning and until recently have been one of a very few instruments of communication. New forms of communication involving a wider use of the senses have found places of importance in learning, along with books. Film strips, moving pictures, recording and playback machines, public address systems, and especially the new forms of television have significant contributions to make in both the educational program and the form of the plant.

Television can make a striking improvement in education. At this time, available equipment is rapidly improving, but experience with it is pitifully limited. Its use in the secondary school is correspondingly limited. Television is not considered here for any use other than improved educational effectiveness. Though it may on occasion extend the voice and person of a teacher from thirty pupils to five hundred, we have chosen to ignore this consideration unless convinced that the five hundred were better taught.

An example of the educational promise of television is seen in the music center. Here it is believed that a single music teacher may direct the work of individuals and small groups working in as many as 20 different practice rooms. The problem of working with this group is solved by means of a closed circuit television system providing communication between the teacher and each of the twenty-odd practice rooms.

Variations of this system are found in all parts of the school plant. The science specialist presents information, conducts experiments, and answers questions from his own science laboratory to one or more teachers and their groups of pupils.

Television makes possible auditory and visual communication between stations located in any part of the entire plant and community. The complex apparatus of the scientist, the insect spraying device of the agricultural shop, and the collection of quartz crystals at the materials center, these and many more are available to any group for viewing and questions.

Television is used, however, only when direct contact and experience is less effective because of size of group, or distance and time problems. Television used by specialists, who are already well known by these students, extends its effectiveness like a telephone call from a friend.

The starting point for the design of this project is the educational program, not the number of square feet per student. Area standards have heretofore been developed by averaging the measurements of existing school buildings. We believe that this approach fails to respond to the most enlightened and forward looking educational philosophy. Every effort has been made to secure the best educational space for meeting carefully determined needs, but no reductions have been made in area at an educational sacrifice.

Neither the building nor the requirements of the program necessitate any departure from existing building codes. Widths of traffic arteries, exits, separation of buildings, and general provisions for fire and panic safety all conform to prevailing building codes.

The student is not regarded as a supervisory problem; areas are not arranged to permit the teacher to have a student continuously within view. Discipline and supervision are best secured by means other than building plan. All decisions as to plan, arrangement, materials, and equipment have been based solely on the implementation of the best educational outcomes and the provision of the most pleasant and stimulating environment.

In the typical secondary school with an enrollment of 1200 students there are approximately 40 to 50 classes in session at any given time. This means that there are 40 to 50 units which require both program and schedule. In this proposed school where there are 1200 students requiring individualized programs, their arrangement and scheduling becomes a matter of astronomical complexity. Each student must have his performance, growth, and personal problems completely documented. A record must be kept of each individual student activity. The operation of this school then will rely heavily on records, and customary systems of record-keeping may prove inadequate. It is anticipated that the use of record keeping and sorting machines such as those found in large business enterprises would be necessary for an operation as complex as that presented by this school. By making use of this modern business equipment, it could be expected that complete records of each student would be quickly available to teachers and the guidance staff.

The buildings are divided into four main groups. Three of these, the Specialized Learnings Center, which is the large square building at the center of the plan; the four home-room units to the east; the Library, Materials Center, Communications, Guidance and Administrative Offices to the south are housed under a uniform roof height providing a clear ceiling height of approximately 12 feet. The fourth, across the northern flank, is the high ceilinged building unit in which are the Auditorium and the Physical Education areas. Between the latter and the main group are the dining facilities with the outdoor theatre directly to the west.

All of the home-room units are the same in plan. There are six home-rooms grouped around a materials center that is a local supply source in which are stored the materials commonly needed in day-to-day work. This is a local center which is augmented by the main materials center at the south of the entire building group. The work shop provides tools and work benches for projects. This shop is distinguished from the shop facilities in the Specialized Learnings Center in that the latter provides a variety of tools for both manual use and power operation which are required for more advanced and complicated projects. Each home-room materials center and shop is serviced by a specialized clerk under the direction of the home-room teacher.

Home-rooms are grouped in pairs with a common office for two teachers and a clerk, with an adjoining conference area. Toilets and space for the storage of outer clothing are shared by pairs of rooms. There are three pairs of home-rooms, six in all, with a capacity of approximately 50 students each. Because of individualized schedules, it is only on rare occasions that fifty students will be in a home-room at one time. Essential to the varied activities carried on in the home-room is the work center desk provided for each student. This may be set up in a number of ways as illustrated on pages 86-87, 103 to meet the requirements of different types of work activity. Since 50 students are seldom in a room at one time, student work tables may be easily disassembled and stored when not in use, thus clearing the area and providing work space for other students.

76

Shared space for out-of-door work is found in the courts between adjacent home-units.

The fullest effectiveness of the learning process is realized when students are selected and grouped in terms of learning purposes. The techniques of grouping are complex. The basic consideration is that students be brought together when a common interest or purpose is discovered. Work and discussion proceed best when these groupings represent not only a common interest but also a cross section of individual traits and characteristics which stimulate discussion and an interplay of ideas and points of view.

Thus the common purpose which binds a group together may be fertilized by a range of individuals of differing social, economic, racial or religious backgrounds. Knowledge and experience in the techniques of analyzing individual educational needs has been developed to a remarkable degree. However, the effective use of such findings has been decidedly limited because of the lack of opportunity for grouping and regrouping pupils for learning experiences in accord with the findings of the guidance process. The considerable body of data that is represented in the student records at the Administrative and Guidance Center, and which is quickly available through sorting machines, makes the formulation of these groups a matter of precision. Buildings are designed to permit the full use of grouping techniques.

In the Specialized Learnings Center are included a variety of activities such as a little theater in which drama and stagecraft are studied, also facilities for business education, mathematics, science, homemaking, arts and crafts, drafting, foreign languages, and music, and a number of shop areas. The proximity of noisy and quiet areas creates a problem in the acoustical treatment of interior space which is difficult but not insoluble.

All of these activities are under a single roof. This gives maximum encouragement for finding related interests. Thus the homemaking room is located near the electrical shop and the woodworking shop in order that the uses of electricity in the home may be explored and studied, and that the construction, design, and maintenance of furniture may be undertaken. Nearby is the arts and crafts studio.

Mathematics and science are closely grouped. Note the provision in the science room for individual student laboratories where special projects may be undertaken for longer periods of time by single students or by small groups. Shops are convenient to the stage area of the little theater. The side walls of the little theater may be opened to extend the action, where required, into a wide arc around the audience area. Foreign languages are located nearby in order that plays may be produced and speakers heard. The music area adjoins the little theater for convenience in the presentation of recitals. Near the little theater and the music center is located an outdoor theater, and across the court is the auditorium. The shop areas, and particularly the automobile and agricultural shops, are situated at the west end of the building in order to provide an outdoor shop yard served from the adjoining street.

The large building to the south houses, on the first floor, the Library and the charging desk for both books and materials which may be taken to the nearby home-rooms or the Specialized Learnings Center by handcart. Also on the ground floor is the television studio. Space is provided in the television studio for the seating of a small audience. Adjoining the television studio are located the guidance offices and the administrative offices for the entire school. Centrally placed is the records room where all student records are quickly available to guidance staff and consultants. Below the ground floor are located a large storage space for books and a large collection of materials and specimens. Deliveries are made to this underground space through loading elevators at the nearby service road. Small service elevators at the center of this building block connect the underground supply area with the charging desks on the ground floor. The small stage in the television studio may be lowered into the Materials Center where materials may be assembled on the stage for telecasts; it may then be raised to the studio floor.

The auditorium seats approximately 1000 people and will be used by both community and student body. At the east end of this building is located the physical education area. The gymnasium provides for a variety of indoor games without space for spectators; exhibition and competitive games will be played in other buildings of the community. Rooms adjacent to the gymnasium floor will be used for special instruction, for class groups, and for audio-visual instruction. Unusual perhaps is the provision of a small bowling alley, a game in which students show considerable interest. The locker-shower room areas are smaller than customarily found in secondary schools since individualized schedules do not create a concentrated congestion for short periods of time.

The dining area provides a variety of accommodations and allows for both cafeteria service and for table service by student waiters. The large dining room is supplemented by smaller dining rooms which may be used for small groups and luncheon committee meetings. A light lunch and sandwich counter offers service to out-of-door diners. Adjoining is a student commons room.

Out-of-door game courts and playfield are adjacent to the physical education center. The location of some of these courts near the dining area encourages light games and play during the luncheon period. The school is the guiding and administering agency of this educational process.

The community is obligated to share actively in the job of educating young people, and its adults are expected to contribute their knowledge and skill. Business and industrial concerns, institutions, churches, parks, community recreational and athletic facilities are all a part of the school plant. The complete plant consists of the school buildings and campus shown here, supplemented by all of the resources and buildings of the community. Young people are a responsible and needed part of such a community.

This plant and this educational program are based on the belief that the community, in the broadest sense of the word, shares with the school the responsibility for education; that this education is essentially a growth and an experience in living, not alone a preparation for it.

PLANS AND SKETCHES

Each school plant is designed to meet a specific program in a certain location and is shaped by the character of the community. Following are drawings which show the school plant evolved from the program requirements outlined in the preceding text. The drawings consist of architectural plans and perspective sketches. It is hoped that the architectural plans will explain the activities housed, the spaces these activities require, and the relationships existing between them.

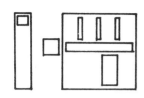

SITE PLAN

A River
B Boathouse
C Play & Game Field
D Parking
E Swimming Pools
F Physical Education Building
G Auditorium
H Paved Game Courts
I Dining & Commons
J Outdoor Theatre
K Home Room Unit
L Special Learnings Building
M Library·Administration·
   Guidance·Counseling·Communications·
   Library Storage·Materials Storage
N Casting Pond
O Game & Recreation Area
P Residential Area
Q Transportation & Building Services
R Delivery & Service Elevators
S Shop Yard
T Service Road
U Outer Drive

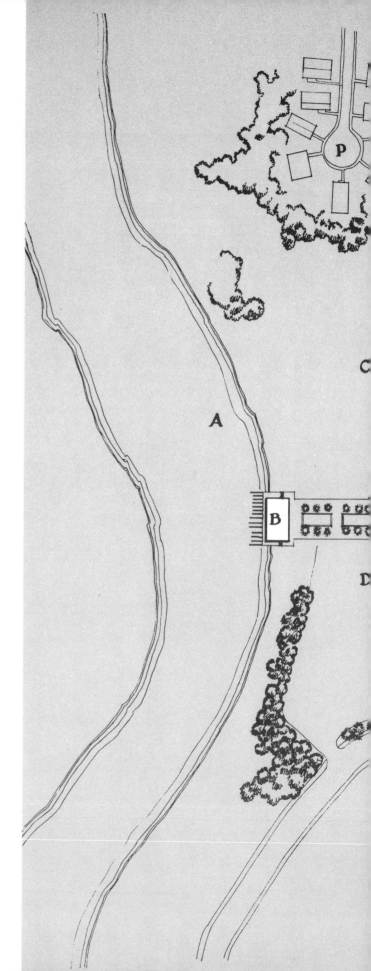

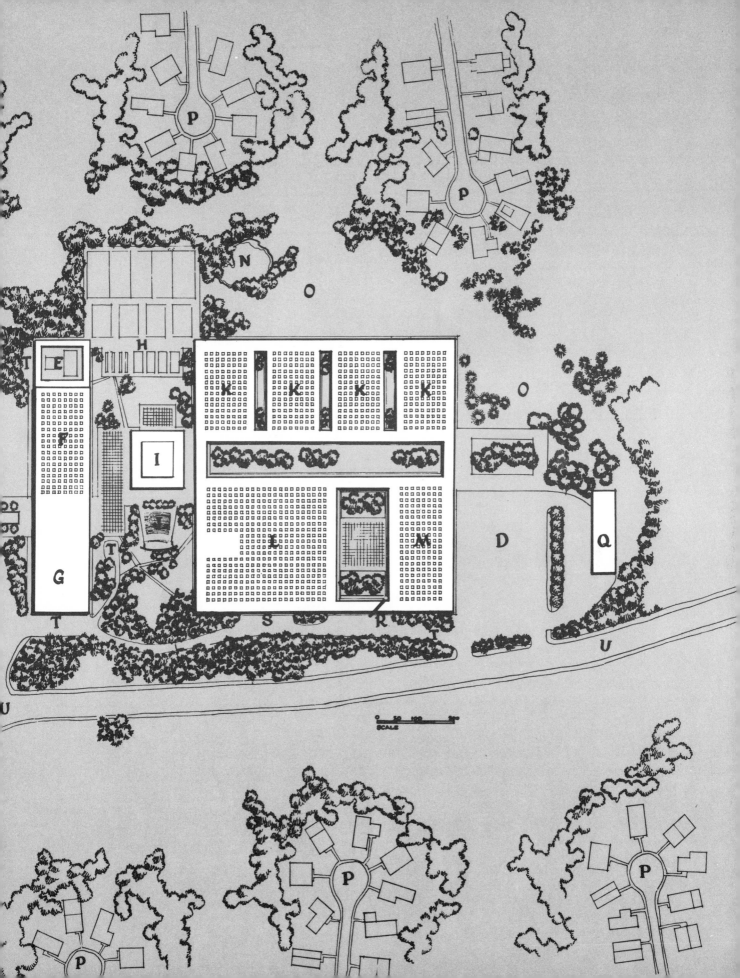

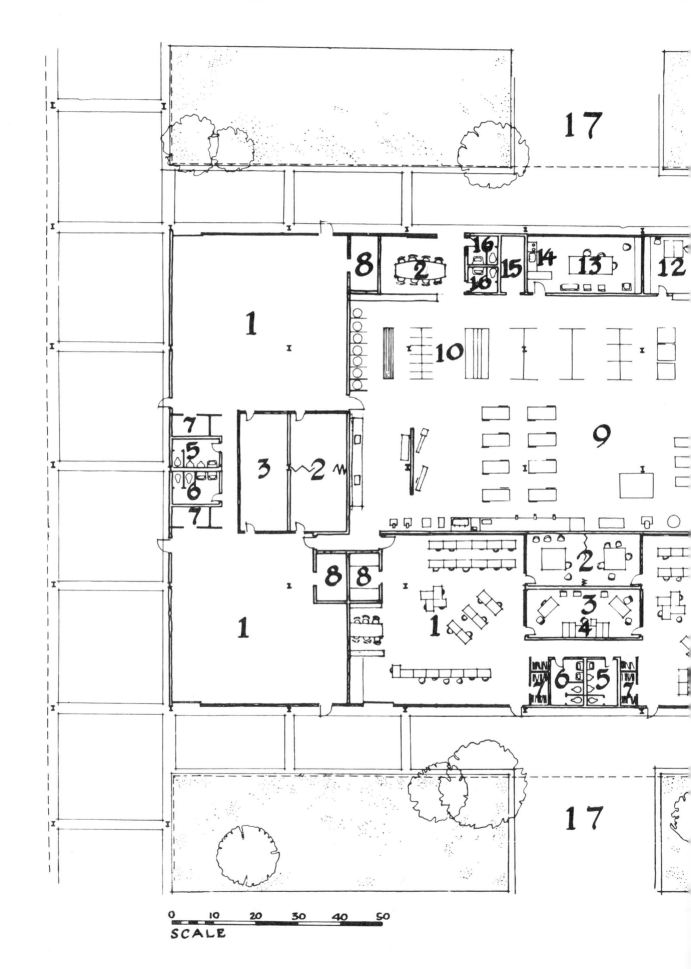

17

8 2

16
16 15 14 13 12

1

10

7
5   9
3 2
6
7

8 8

1 2

1 3
4

7 6 5 7

17

0   10   20   30   40   50
SCALE

86

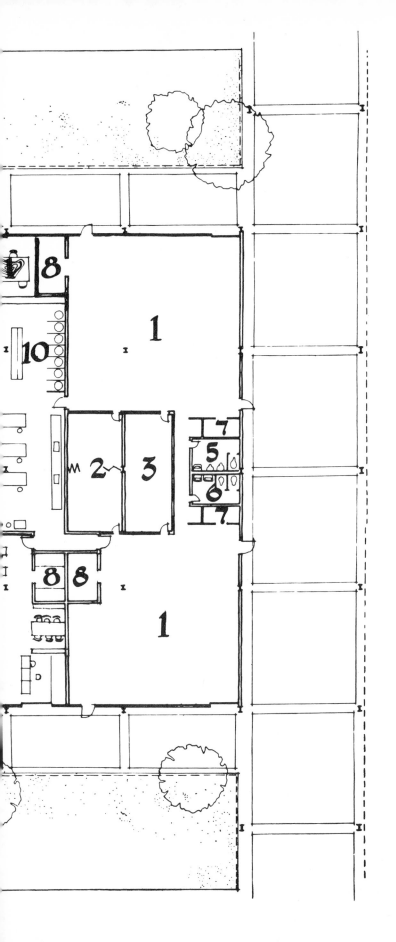

HOME ROOM UNIT

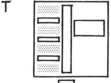

1	Home Room
2	Conference
3	Teachers' Room
4	Clerk
5	Boys' Toilet
6	Girls' Toilet
7	Wardrobe
8	Student Desk Storage
9	Project Shop & Work Area
10	Materials Storage
11	Conference & Special Projects
12	Materials & Shop Clerk
13	Teachers' Conference & Work Area
14	Kitchenette
15	Mechanical Equipment
16	Teachers' Toilet
17	Court

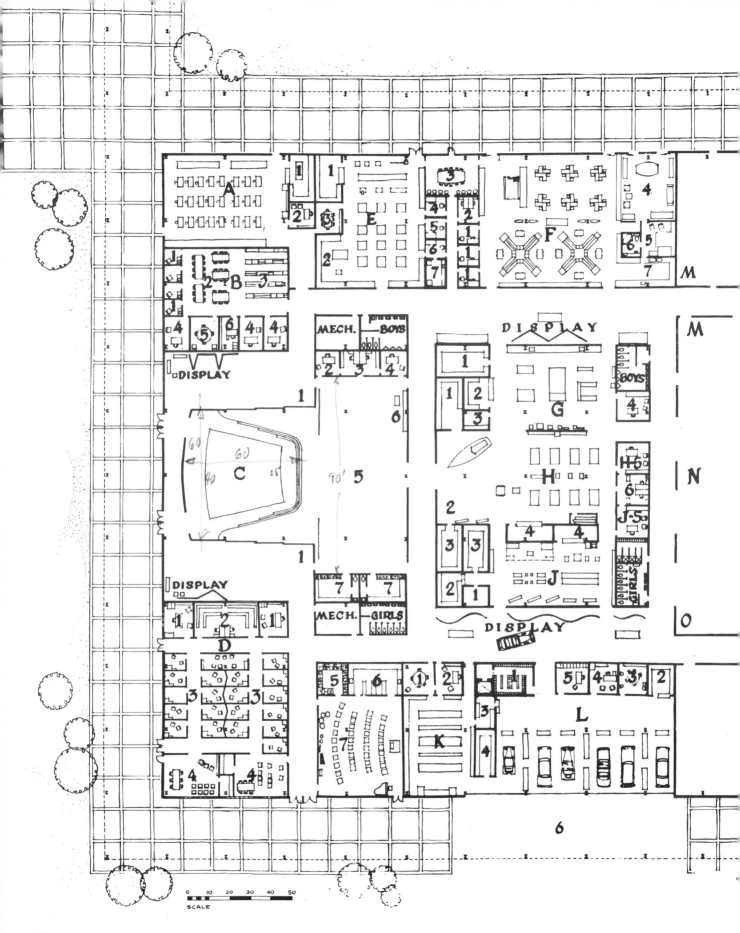

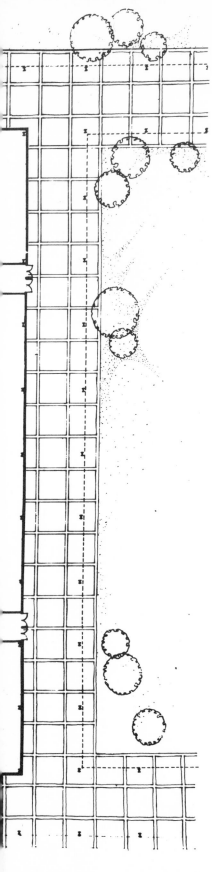

SPECIAL LEARNINGS BUILDING

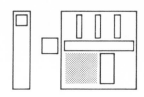

A Draughting
1 Supply & Printing
2 Draughting Specialist
3 Conference

B Foreign Languages
1 Listening & Study Cubicles
2 Work Area
3 Books & Audio-Visual Materials
4 Foriegn Language Specialist
5 Conference
6 Clerk

C Little Theatre
seating capacity 325
1 Side Stage
2 Stagecraft Specialist
3 Clerk
4 Drama Specialist
5 Stage Platform
6 Work Area
7 Dressing Room

D Music
1 Music Specialist
2 Clerk & Library
3 Practice Rooms
4 Group Listening-Conference-Practice
5 Wardrobe
6 Instrument Storage
7 Instrumental & Choral Room

E Arts and Crafts
1 Supply
2 Printing
3 Conference
4 Arts & Crafts Specialist
5 Clerk
6 Photography Specialist
7 Dark Room

F Homemaking
1 Homemaking Specialist
2 Clerk
3 Conference

4 Living Room
5 Bed Room
6 Bath Room
7 Utility Area

G Electrical Shop
1 Project Storage
2 Tools
3 Radio Room
4 Electrical Shop Specialist

H Woodworking Shop
1 Finishing
2 Project Area
3 Project Storage
4 Supply
H·5 Woodworking Shop Specialist
6 Clerk

J Metals Shop
1 Finishing
2 Tools
3 Project Storage
4 Supply
J·5 Metals Shop Specialist
6 Clerk

K Agriculture
1 Conference & Library
2 Agriculture Specialist
3 Laboratory
4 Storage

L Automotive Shop
1 Lockers & Showers
2 Parts
3 Conference & Library
4 Automotive Specialist
5 Clerk
6 Shop Yard

M Science

N Mathematics

O Business Education

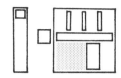

SPECIAL LEARNINGS BUILDING

A   Draughting

B   Foreign Languages

C   Little Theatre

D   Music

E   Arts and Crafts

F   Homemaking
 1   Homemaking Specialist
 2   Clerk
 3   Conference
 4   Living Room
 5   Bed Room
 6   Bathroom
 7   Utility Area

G   Electrical Shop
 1   Project Storage
 2   Tools
 3   Radio Room
 4   Electrical Shop Specialist

H   Woodworking Shop
 1   Finishing
 2   Project Area
 3   Project Storage
 4   Supply
 H·5   Woodworking Shop Specialist
 6   Clerk

J   Metals Shop
 1   Finishing
 2   Tools
 3   Project Storage
 4   Supply
 J·5   Metals Shop Specialist
 6   Clerk

K   Agriculture
 1   Conference & Library
 2   Agricultural Specialist
 3   Laboratoratory
 4   Storage

L   Automotive Shop
 1   Lockers and Showers
 2   Parts
 3   Conference & Library
 4   Automotive Specialist
 5   Clerk
 6   Shop Yard

M   Science
 1   Conference
 2   Chemistry Storage
 3   Preparation
 4   Physics Storage
 5   Student Project Laboratory
 6   Lecture Room
 7   Science Specialist
 8   Specialists' Laboratory
 9   Conference

N   Mathematics
 1   Clerk
 2   Group Instruction Work Area
 N·3   Mathematics Specialist
 4   Conference

O   Business Education
 1   Clerk
 2   Group Instruction Work Area
 O·3   Business Education Specialist
 4   Conference
 5   Typing
 6   Business Machine Instruction
 7   Business Machine Laboratory

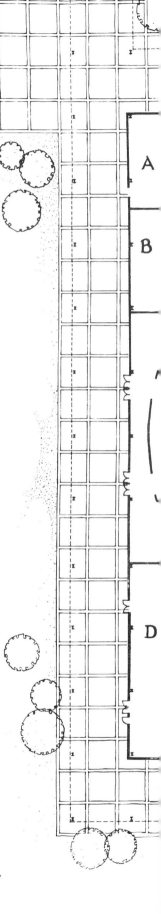

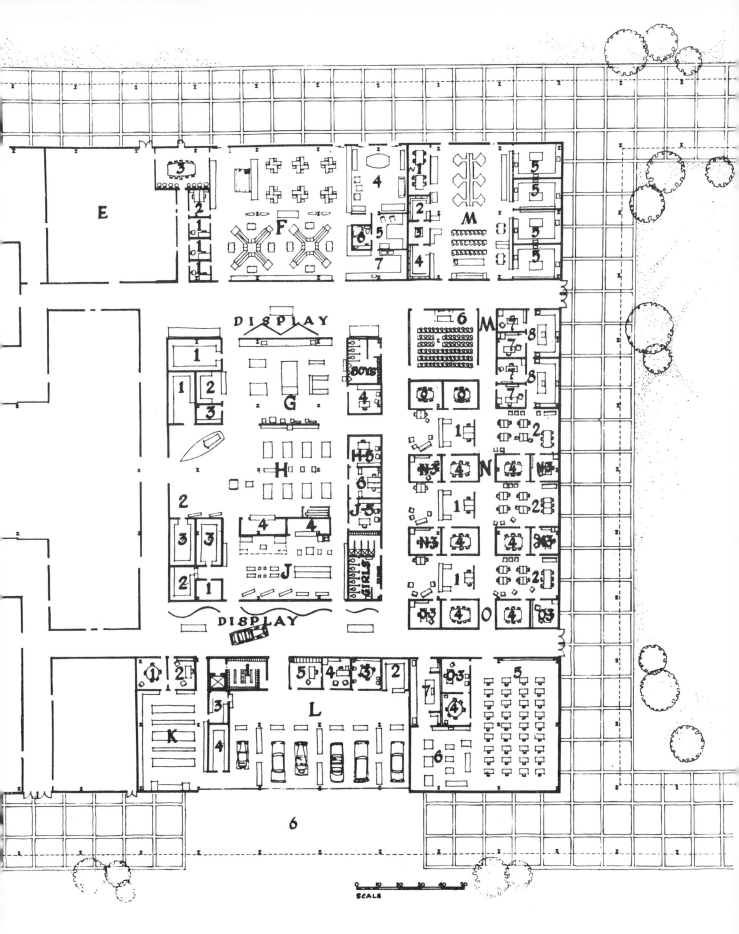

E

3

2
1
1

F

4

1
2

4
6 5
7

M

5
5
5
5

DISPLAY

1

1 2

3

G

2

3 3

2 1

J

H

BOYS
4

H 5

6

J 5

GIRLS

DISPLAY

6

1

2

N 3

4

N

4

N 3

1

2

N 3

4

4

N 3

1

2

N 3

4

4

N 3

O 3

4

4

O 3

O

6

M

7

7

7

7

8

8

K

1

2

3

4

L

5

4

3

2

3

7

3

4

6

5

6

SCALE

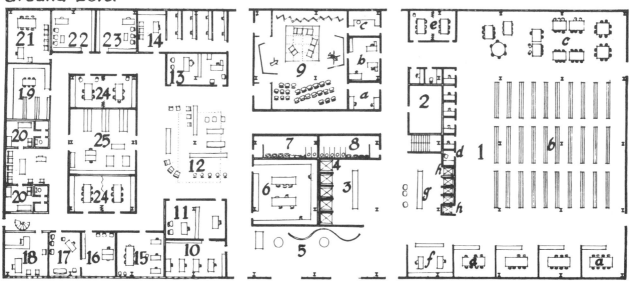

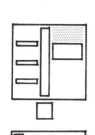

LIBRARY- ADMINISTRATION - GUIDANCE
COUNSELLING - COMMUNICATIONS

1	Library	3	Materials Center Charging Desk
a	Special Study Rooms	4	Service Elevators
b	Book Stacks	5	Display
c	Reading and Study	6	Workroom
d	Study Carrels	7	Boys' Toilet
e	Conference	8	Girls' Toilet
f	Librarian	9	Television Studio
g	Book charging Desk	a	Public Relations
h	Service Elevator	b	Studio Direction
2	Mechanical Equipment	c	Illustrator
		10	Curriculum & Test Materials Writing
		11	Curriculum Director
		12	Waiting Area

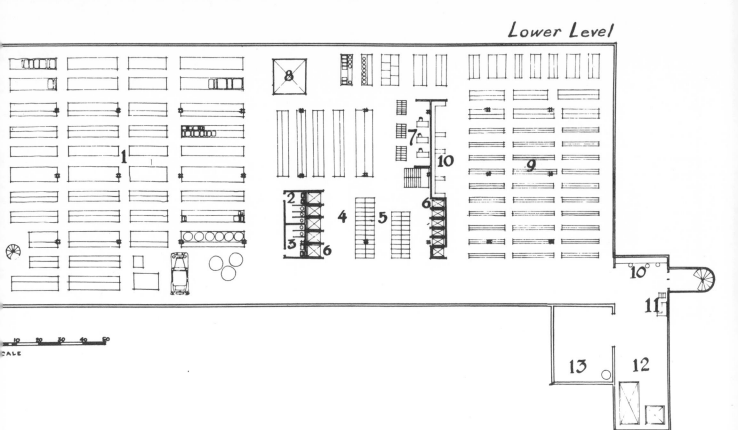

LIBRARY STORAGE AND MATERIALS STORAGE

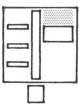

13	Guidance	1	Materials Storage
14	Psychometrist	2	Women's Toilet
15	Student Council	3	Men's Toilet
16	Bursar - Bookkeeping	4	Sorting & Delivery Area
17	Vice Principal	5	Carts
18	Principal	6	Service Elevator
19	Professional Library	7	Clerks
20	Nurse	8	Television Service Elevator
21	Occupation Information	9	Library Storage
22	Girls' Counsellor	10	Work Area
23	Boys' Counsellor	11	Clerk
24	Conference	12	Service Elevator - Receiving Area
25	Records - Clerical	13	Mechanical

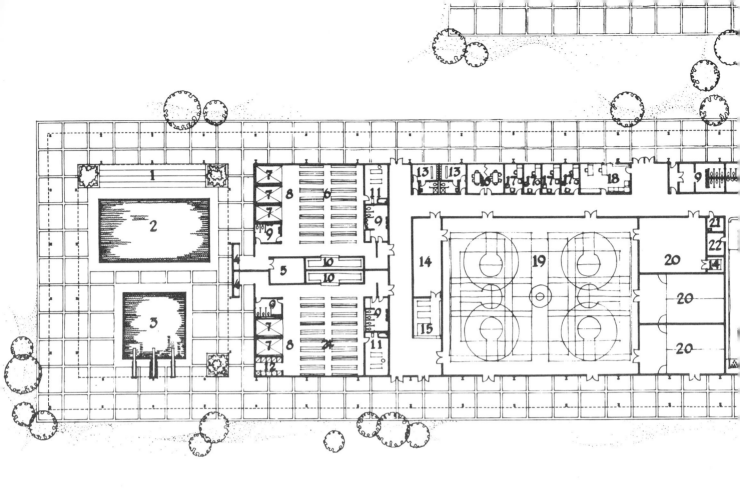

PHYSICAL EDUCATION BUILDING

1	Spectators	13	Staff Lockers & Shower
2	Instruction Pool	14	Storage
3	Diving Pool	15	Field Equipment
4	Pool Equipment Storage	16	Conference
5	Mechanical Equipment	17	Physical Education Specialist
6	Boys' Locker Room	18	Clerk & Reception
7	Group Showers	19	Gymnasium
8	Drying area	20	Special Exercise - Classroom - Games
9	Toilet	21	Custodial storage
10	Towels & Storage	22	Bowling Equipment & Storage
11	Therapy	23	Bowling Alleys
12	Individual Showers	24	Girls' Locker Room

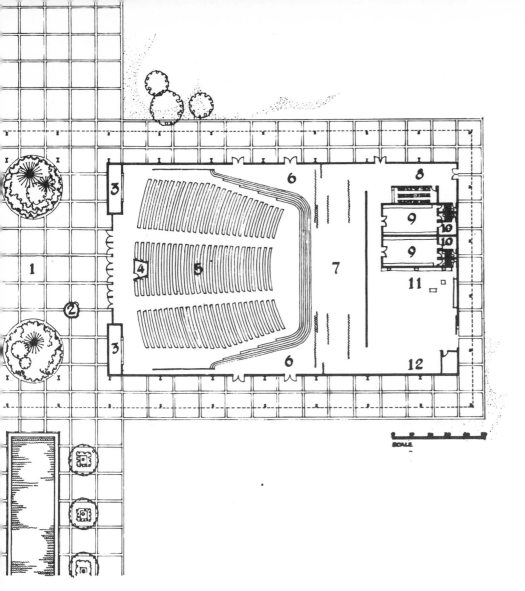

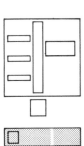

AUDITORIUM

1 Loggia
2 Tickets
3 Storage & Check Rooms
4 Projection Booth
5 Auditorium - seating capacity 1000
6 Side stage
7 Stage platform
8 Wardrobe storage & Work room
9 Group Dressing Room
10 Individual Dressing Room
11 Stagecraft Shop Work Area
12 Set Storage

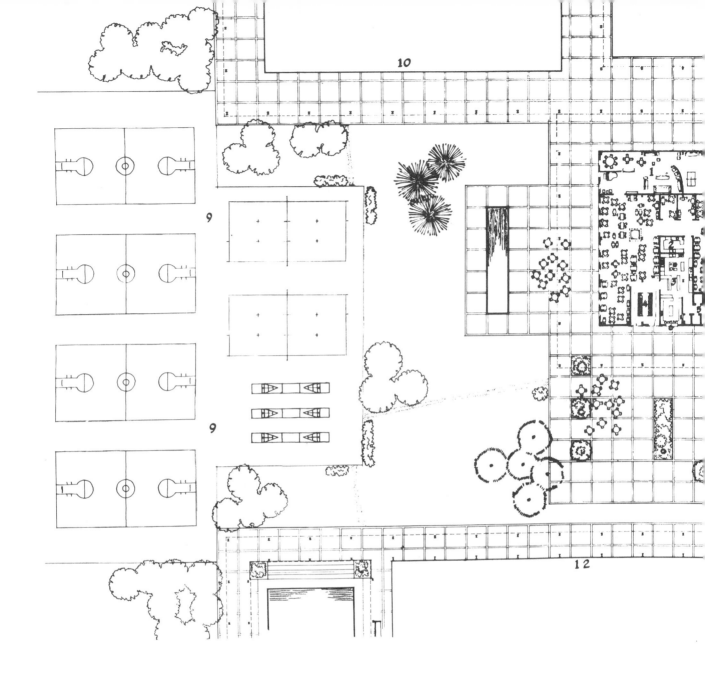

DINING & COMMONS BUILDING

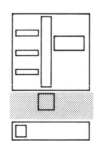

1   Commons Room
2   Scullery
3   Kitchen
4   Serving Counters
5   Delivery & Storage
6   Snack Bar
7   Service Road

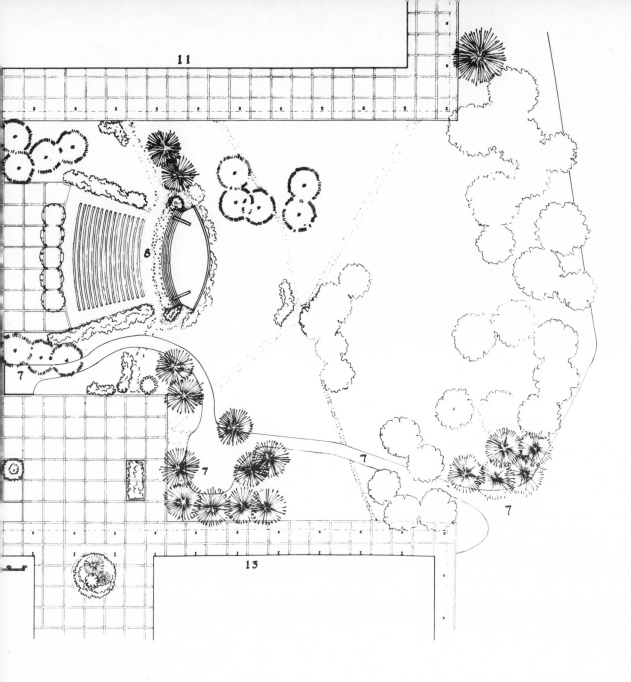

8   *Outdoor Theatre*

9   *Paved Game Courts*

10   *Home Room Unit*

11   *Special Learnings Bldg.*

12   *Physical Education Building*

13   *Auditorium*

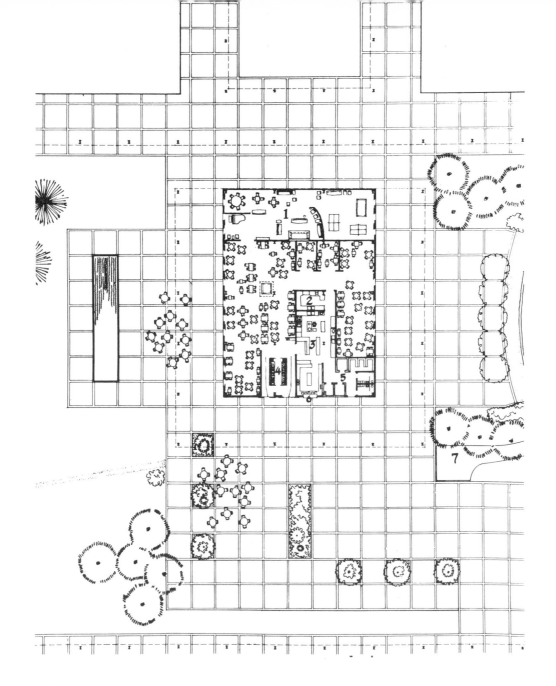

DINING & COMMONS BUILDING

1   Commons Room

2   Scullery

3   Kitchen

4   Serving Counters

5   Delivery & Storage

6   Snack Bar

7   Service Road

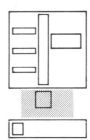

The following illustrations are designed to convey an understanding of the environment and uses of the school plant. Considerations of building materials, matters of engineering and construction have been subordinated in order that the plant in use may have first claim on the reader's attention.

The school plant finds itself in a park-like setting. A residential vehicular artery in the foreground provides access to parking and service areas. The river is in the left background. The residential areas in the center background are penetrated by fingers of park, recreation and game areas extending outward from the school plant.

Court between Home Room
Buildings. This Court provides open areas of light, air
and planting and is used for
projects such as the accumulation and recording of weather
data and the construction of a
masonry garden wall. Two
carts with materials from the
main Materials Center are in
evidence.

Home Room. Behind the glass wall at center are the Teacher's Room and the Conference Room. Wardrobes and toilet rooms at left background. Rooms are designed for a wide variety of study and work activity.

Home Room. Periodical and Reference Area and small work counter are located in each Home Room.

Shop and Materials Center in Home Room Building. A variety of materials normally required for day to day use are stored in cabinets and shelves at left. At far left are located Teacher's Work Room and Office for Clerk-Supervisor. This Shop provides work tables and benches for light craft and shop work normally a part of class projects.

Office for Home Room Teachers and Clerk. This Office serves two Home Rooms, with facilities for two teachers and a clerk serving both.

The Student Work Desk is an item of furniture which is of great importance to the operation of the school. One of these desks is provided for each student in the school and it becomes his base of operations for all of his activities in the school plant and the surrounding community. It provides for a wide variety of use and work and it may be used singly or in many combinations, some of which are shown in the following illustrations.

This desk belongs to the student for the full school year, or perhaps for 4 years. In addition to being a work center, it is a permanent storage unit where he may store materials for long periods of time. When the student is away from the Home Room on a work assignment, the cabinet pedestal is stored in the Home Room, the component parts are stored in the Home Room Materials Center. The pedestal unit occupies 1'x 2' of floor space, or when stacked in pairs, the equivalent of 6"x 2' floor space.

screw holes at top

Cabinet -opens from back— miscellaneous storage of glue, poster paint, drafting equipment, etc.

Drawer - 8½"x 11" paper, separate trays for each of 3 colors, pencil, pens, clips, etc.

Typewriter shelf.

Letter File Drawer.

Shelf— open at both ends for 18" roll of tracing paper, T square and triangles.

This is the appearance of the other side of the desk pedestal unit. A is a single piece of material 23"x24", with 4 screw holes in which are used screws with a coin slot. One side of A is a work surface, the other side is cork pinning board.

cork surface this side

If a student desires, he may detach A by unscrewing the 4 screws, and,

1. he may raise it to the next set of holes and re-fasten with screws providing a vertical cork surface towards the pedestal. (Left)

2. he may place the A piece horizontally on the pedestal unit providing a small work table or desk. (Right)

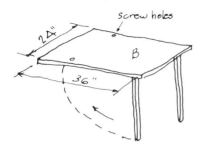

screw holes

24"

B

36"

This is piece B which is a desk top unit. When not in use it is stored at the Home Unit Materials Center. With the legs extended it is screwed to the top of the pedestal unit. The legs fold and lock into position as in a good quality bridge table.

The component parts of the student desk may be assembled in these combinations:

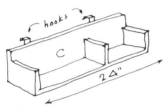

hooks

C

24"

This is piece C which is a book shelf unit. It is obtainable when needed and upon requisition from the Home Unit Materials Center. It hooks over the edge of the A unit.

36" 24"

B

A

A and B are thus assembled into the most commonly used form.

B

A

The Typewriter Shelf may drawn out for typing.

C

A

B

The book shelf unit C may be hooked over A when needed.

A

B

The cork surface of A may be used for pinning up papers and notes. It may be used as a barrier or screen against adjacent desks.

Four students may
work together

or

two students.

desks may be joined
to provide a larger
work surface.

Television is widely used in this school plant as an extension to the effectiveness of the teacher. Some of the more typical uses of television are suggested by this group of illustrations.

The Science Specialist is presenting a lecture on chemistry which is televised to the various parts of the school plant and, in some cases, to the community. This telecast originates in the Laboratory of the Science Specialist.

This telecast is received by a small group of students in one of the Home Rooms. It is possible for this Home Room group to question the Science Specialist and to discuss or develop the subject matter by an exchange of comments and questions.

Another larger group in a different part of the school plant may listen to the lecture by means of a projected screen image, and listen to the conversational exchange.

The Television Studio is used for televising a wide variety of subject matter as well as small dramatic presentations. A section of the studio floor may be dropped to the Materials Center immediately below, where the resource materials in the Materials Center may be placed on the platform and raised into place, which facilitates the handling of the wide variety of resources available. There are provisions for a small audience.

The Music Specialist from his office may view and hear approximately twenty practice rooms nearby in his department, where both individuals and small groups are practicing.

In the Special Learnings Area
the group of two clerks in the
center serves for Mathematics
Specialists in nearby rooms.
Two of the rooms at the left
are cut away to show, at far
left, the Office of the Mathematics Specialist, and a Conference Room immediately
adjoining. In the left background and on the right are
three other groups, each containing a similar Office and
Conference Room. Over the
screen behind the two clerks
is a small Work and Waiting
Area, which on occasion may
serve as a classroom or lecture
area for small groups.

The Charging and Delivery Desk at the main Materials Center. Elevators behind the desk connect to the Materials and Book Storage Area below and are used for transporting, issuing and returning carts to and from other parts of the plant. A Catalog File for the available materials in the Materials Center is in the foreground. There are similar facilities opposite this for issuing and returning books and periodicals.

The Materials Center. Here are stored a vast quantity of materials used widely in all parts of the school plant. Elevators connecting directly with the Delivery Desk above are at center.

Carts are loaded by clerks to fill requisitions placed at the Delivery Desk on the floor above.

The Records Room. Here are kept detailed records of work assignments, student performance, student traits, all of which are available to the teaching staff and consulting specialists and counsellors. This vast body of data is sorted by electronic sorting machines and made available to those desiring information on the students.

The Little Theater in the Special Learnings Center features a platform which extends not only across the front of the theater but also along the two sides of the seating area. The side arms of the platform may be widened into the adjoining display and circulation areas; a platform that invites experimentation by the imaginative Drama Specialist. When desired, the action may envelop the spectator, making him feel that he is a participant.

The Auditorium seats approximately one thousand people.
As in the Little Theater, the
platform extends widely
around the audience area.
The illustration is intended to
show the wide use of this platform that is possible.

This is the main Dining Room in the Dining Area. Serving lines for cafeteria service are at the left. A nearby door into the Kitchen makes it possible to serve directly from the Kitchen to the diners when desired.

There are Dining Rooms available to large and small groups who may desire to meet at meal time.

The Commons Room provides for recreation, reading, conversation and games. This closely adjoins the Dining Areas.

The Dining Area Building also serves those who may wish to eat out of doors in favorable weather; it adjoins the Open Air Theater at background right.

A large area between the Auditorium, left, and the Physical Education Building, right, serves for informal gatherings during inclement weather.

The Swimming Pools. A constant depth pool is in the foreground, with a deeper diving pool at right. The Locker Rooms and the Physical Education Building are at center background.

The Esplanade connecting the Lobby Area between the Physical Education Buildings and Auditorium leads to the Boat House in the background.

INDEX